IMAGES OF Farnham

IMAGES OF Farnham

The Breedon Books
Publishing Company
Derby

First published in Great Britain by
The Breedon Books Publishing Company Limited
44 Friar Gate, Derby, DE1 1DA.
1997

ISBN 1 85983 090 0

Printed and bound by Butler & Tanner, Frome, Somerset.
Jacket printed by Lawrence Allen Ltd, Weston-super-Mare, Somerset.
Colour film by RPS Ltd of Leicester.

Contents

Introduction
6

Long, Long Ago...
8

The Knight Years
11

Village Life
23

That's Entertainment
53

It Pays To Advertise
64

Accidents Will Happen
67

On The Streets Where You Lived
75

The Shopping Experience
89

Schooldays Remembered
97

Some Special Occasions
109

Working Days
125

Sporting Life
152

People and Places
169

Subscribers
188

Introduction

By Peter Thompson, Editor, Farnham Herald

I HAD twin objectives in preparing this book. One was to nourish an affection for the past by showing the face of Farnham and its villages over the decades.

The other was to capture the essential spirit of the town through its people – hence the marked human dimension to the spread of pictures.

The book has no formal structure; it makes no claims to being a precise historical document; other, more scholarly publications, have performed that task with marked success.

The book is, above all, a celebration; a pictorial salute to a jewel of a town perched on Surrey's borders with Hampshire.

For local government purposes, Farnham is part of Waverley. County Hall in Kingston holds sway in other spheres.

Despite being beholden in legislative terms, Farnham remains fiercely independent of spirit; proud of its rich panoply of architecture, proud of its many clubs and organisations, proud of its thriving arts community and proud of its record in charity works.

The town owed its growth to the development of agriculture in mediæval times. The manor was given to the Bishops of Winchester in 688 by King Caedwalla of Wessex. After the Norman Conquest a Norman bishop, Henry of Blois, built a castle on the London to Winchester road. It became the Palace of the Bishops of Winchester. Today we know it more simply as Farnham Castle. The 12th-century stone keep, the walls and a fine Tudor tower remain to attract visitors today.

In wide and handsome Castle Street, many of the homes boast Georgian fronts on mediæval buildings, identified by steeply pitched roofs. But don't linger here too long, tempting though it is. A wealth of architectural gems awaits the visitor prepared to roam the streets and cobbled yards of the town.

For the more adventurous, Farnham Park, set above the town, offers wide open spaces for walking as well as outstanding views.

The Maltings, an arts and community centre, is the envy of many other towns. It is also testimony to what can be achieved when the energy of a community is harnessed.

The Museum of Farnham, on West Street, is another success story, not least in the manner it has forged links with schools.

William Cobbett, radical politician and author of *Rural Rides*, was born at the Jolly Farmer Inn, now the William Cobbett, in Bridge Square.

George Sturt, a passionate chronicler of rural life, John Henry Knight of early motoring fame, and Mike Hawthorn, world motor racing champion, are other names indelibly linked to Farnham.

Jonathan Swift, too, was at his productive best while living at Moor Park on the outskirts of the town.

Time and progress has not always been kind to Farnham. Like all towns of its age, it has met problems in preserving the best of its heritage while accommodating the needs of the present. In the last 50 years this has become a precarious balancing act. The

Farnham Society, ever vigilant against those whose ambitions make them less appreciative of the architectural heritage, is dedicated to preserving the beauty and dignity of the town.

As a relative newcomer, I often try to imagine how life would have been in these streets before they succumbed to the remorseless advance of the motor car. To pedestrianise or not is the recurring question, and one to which an answer must be provided sooner rather than later.

But Farnham does not allow itself to be dragged down by these concerns. Neither does it wallow in the past, or fret about the future. I see it alert, vibrant, always trying to present an attractive face to the world; I witness its independent traders mounting a challenge to the big guns of commerce; I witness it developing as one of the county's major centres for dining out.

I see youngsters from the Surrey Institute of Art Design adding their rich array of colours to the fabric of life in the town.

Visit the town in summer and be ready to be bowled over by the efforts of the Farnham in Bloom team as they add to their long list of successes.

As I look to the villages I see a thriving community spirit. I see old traditions being sustained by a new generation of village folk mindful of their past; a generation willing to contribute to the seasonal rituals, whether it be cricket matches, fêtes, flower shows or any of the other bastions of village life.

The *Herald* has been at the heart of Farnham for more than 100 years, reporting, recording and helping to sustain a belief in the community ethos.

The bulk of these photographs have been drawn from the pages of the *Herald*.

My thanks to those who provided the balance, or allowed me to tap into their knowledge of the town, in particular Maurice Hewins, Geoff Lunn, John Chuter, Alexa Barrow and Monica Jones.

Welcome, then, to *Images of Farnham*. Enjoy this journey into the past and may you encounter many old friends.

Long, Long Ago...

The St Andrew's parish church, from a lithograph published by Messrs Nichols about 1852.

The castle and Castle Street 200 years ago, an engraving by Fitler from an original drawing by E.T.Burney.

Old Market House, which stood at the bottom of Castle Street. This is dated 1850.

Resting place of a famous son. The tomb of William Cobbett, radical politician and author, in the St Andrew's churchyard.

Let's go the fair ...the scene in Castle Street in 1884.

A drawing by Anabella Harriette Harkness, showing Castle Street in 1869. (Loaned to the *Herald* by Paul Croxson.)

The Knight Years

John Henry Knight,(1847-1917), was one of the great characters of Victorian Farnham. He was born at Weybourne House into an important family, who owned the local bank~brewery interests and several farms. Although his parents hoped he would enter the church, Knight had other ideas. After being taught by the curate at Hale and at a boarding school in Southampton, he trained as an engineer at Deptford.

John Henry's father had died when he was only nine and on completing his articles at 21, he came into his inheritance. For a time he farmed his Badshot estate and became one of Farnham's 'hop barons'. He was keen on the new productive 'high farming' methods, which enabled him to apply his engineering skills. Knight was wealthy enough to take risks and developed a steam powered hop rigger in 1874. However, his reputation as an engineer rests on a best-selling paraffin oil engine produced in the 1890s. With his wife, Elizabeth, who he married in 1884, John Henry built Barfield at Runfold as a state of the art home, complete with electric light. There, they raised a happy family of five children.

In 1895, Knight gained national fame as a member of a pressure group campaigning to change the 'Red Flag Act'. His little car was intended to demonstrate how silly the law was. In many ways, though, his best legacy to Farnham was his collection of photographs.

John Henry Knight as depicted in Alfred Eggar's reminiscences published around 1912. In the original caption he is incorrectly attributed with being the inventor of the first English motor car. 'Knighty' (see later) is now thought to have been the fourth car to run on English roads.

During his lifetime, Knight lived in several houses around Farnham, but the two best known are Weybourne House and Barfield at Runfold. Weybourne House (shown here) was the family home and it was to here he returned after completing his apprenticeship. Complete with a fully equipped workshop, the house provided adequate resources for John Henry to indulge his inventive passion.

The Knight camera recorded this view of the magnificent stand of horse chestnut trees providing a leafy arbour in the gardens of Weybourne House. Today the house has been split up into flats and the gardens likewise.

In 1884, John Henry married Elizabeth Foley at East Wickham in Kent. Later they returned to Farnham to raise their family in a house at Runfold which was being built for them. This was Barfield, now a school, and while the building work was in progress the couple lived in Thumblands, just down the road, in order that Knight could keep a close eye on the work. Barfield, shown here soon after completion in 1888, was to become the setting for the product of much of the inventor's genius to see the light of day.

John Henry Knight's name is always associated with early motoring, but his interest in transport goes back many years before this. Here he is seen aboard an Invincible two-track roadster made by the Surrey Machinists Company around 1892. However, it was in 1869 that John Henry bought his first machine, a Velocipede built in Coventry and commonly referred to as the 'boneshaker'.

While living at Weybourne, Knight engaged the services of a fitter, a carpenter and a lad to help with work on his first big project. Word soon leaked out that a steam road carriage was under construction. So it was that a small crowd had gathered on 2 September 1868 to witness the first trial run. Knight came out of the gates of Weybourne House only to crash into the bank opposite. Undeterred he backed out and set off along the road for some 500 yards before two spokes failed, resulting in the vehicle being towed home by a horse. Later, speeds of 8mph were reached while towing a pony chaise with three passengers. Even then, though, trials were not without incident. On several occasions the vehicle ended up going through hedges into the local hopfields. All the trials were against the law because the Locomotive Act required a man with a red flag to precede the vehicle which itself should be licensed.

John Henry and wife Elizabeth aboard 'Knighty' at Barfield, probably during late 1895. This is Knight's car in its early three-wheeled version. The design of a car came about as a result of a visit to M.Serpollet's works in Montmartre, Paris, in 1893 during which Knight saw, and rode on, an early motor vehicle. While one of the earliest cars in this country, it is now generally recognised that 'Knighty' was not the first. It does, however, hold the distinction of being the first car stopped by the police. Driver James Pullinger was charged, along with Knight, following an incident in Castle Street on 17 October 1895. He was charged with using a vehicle without a licence and outside of permitted hours.

Following Knight's death in 1917, the famous car suffered somewhat mixed fortunes. It eventually came into the care of the Farnham Urban District Council who allowed it to become neglected in a garage of their South Street offices. In 1949 it was moved across the road to the showroom of Heath & Wiltshire's garage for an exhibition. While on the short journey across the highway, George Parfitt took the opportunity to climb aboard for a photograph to be taken. Back in 1895 it was George who had carried out most of the work in producing the car at Elliott's Reliance Works in West Street, under Knight's direction. As can be seen, by this time the car was in a sorry state. The Knight family later ensured the vehicle's survival by asking for it to go to the newly-created Montagu Motor Museum at Beaulieu in the early 1950s.

During the Knight years, Barfield saw many early motor cars, but probably never more at once than on Good Friday 1898. On that day John Henry entertained members of the newly-formed Automobile Club during their first run. The organisation later became the RAC and continues to uphold the rights of the motorist much as Knight did in his day.

The high cost of rubber vehicle tyres much concerned John Henry. So much so in fact that in 1911 he patented a wooden tyre built up of strips of ash. The wood was made springy by a number of parallel cuts in the end of each piece. A limited company was formed with shares sold to friends and relatives, and two of the tyres were fitted to a lorry. This was driven around Runfold by Knight's daughter Ella and her brothers, and was apparently very noisy. The idea did not catch on despite the motoring press suggesting the design might have a future with the army. A model of the tyre still exists in the collection of the Museum of Farnham.

Most of John Henry Knight's inventions made him little money. However, there was one which reversed this trend. In 1889 he designed a small oil engine, running on paraffin, which was designed for such purposes as driving agricultural machinery and lighting country houses. Knight held the patent with a Mr Weyman and it was marketed as the 'Trusty', several hundred being produced of a variety of sizes, some by other manufacturers such as Clayton & Shuttleworth. This particularly large example, produced by Weyman & Hitchcock of Guildford, has been trailer-mounted to assist manoeuvrability and Knight can be seen on the extreme left.

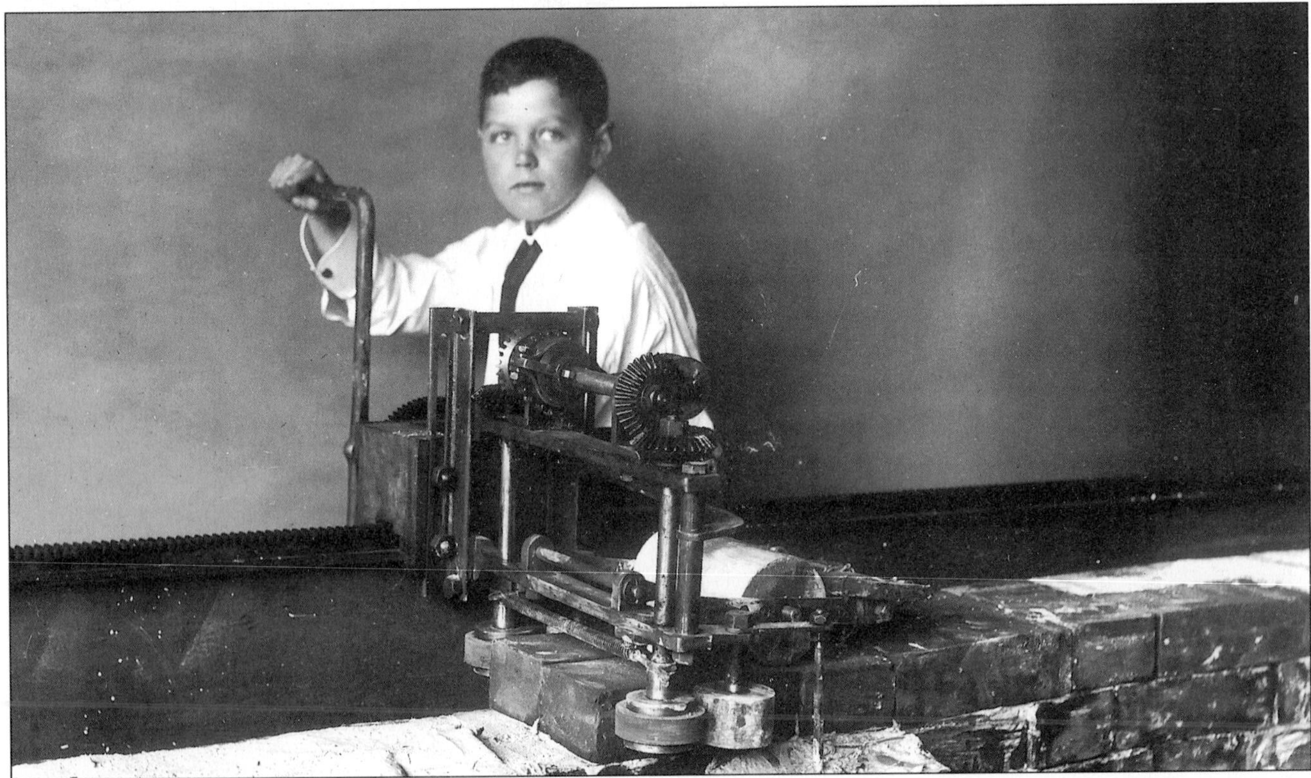

This photograph shows one of John Henry's least successful inventions being demonstrated at Barfield. The machine was described in *The Engineer* in 1902. This was an attempt at a machine to lay bricks, however, it required the setting up of a horizontal beam along which the machine would run, and then the services of two men and a boy. As can be seen, the boy was required to turn the handle while the men laid the mortar and fed the bricks. Knight claimed that it could lay 600 bricks per hour, but, although it completed this wall at Barfield House, it was not a success, probably largely due to the fact that the machine could not turn corners.

An appeal from General Jackson at the Ministry of Munitions during World War One, for people to devise ways of helping our men in the trenches, led to what, probably, was Knight's last invention. With all the look of a piece dating from the days of mediæval siege warfare, he designed this catapult to throw Mills bombs several hundred yards. Years before, John Henry had studied and lectured on the siege engines of the Greeks and Romans, so the chance to put his researches to a practical test appealed to him. This machine, thought to be one of at least three different versions built in Elliott's Reliance works in West Street during 1915, is shown during tests behind the works overlooking what later became the Memorial Ground, which, according to eyewitnesses, the projectiles cleared with ease.

All the inventive genius of the man required substantial investments of capital to maintain. This was largely generated by the family's agricultural interests at Badshot Farm. His bailiff was a Mr Cable who looked after the day-to-day running of the enterprise, which was dairy and arable farm with a considerable area given over to hop growing. Knight, the early photographer, recorded many farming scenes, including this seed drill at work alongside the railway on a site that is now a cemetery.

In the latter years of the 19th century, when Knight was using a 12 x 10ins plate camera, agriculture was still fairly labour intensive. Here the threshing crew are at work beside the large elm tree at Weybourne from which the present day public house takes its name. Later, members of the farm workforce were drafted in to help with his inventions. Foremost among these was James Pullinger, who went on to drive the motor car and subsequently ended up in the magistrates' court alongside his employer. In this scene it is believed to be Pullinger who is in charge of the stationary steam engine standing on the extreme left.

The 'agriculture to support inventions' wasn't a one-way trade, however. Here one of the Trusty oil engines is seen at work driving a chaff cutter, under the close scrutiny of John Henry Knight in the centre.

Idyllic traffic-free conditions are recorded by the Knight camera in this *c.*1880 view of Castle Street. As yet the street, save for the cobbled area stretching up from the clock-towered Corn Exchange building, is unsurfaced. The gothic building which dominates the scene is Knight's Bank. Owned by John Henry's forbears and his branch of the family were fortunately unaffected by its subsequent decline and takeover by the Capital & Counties in 1886. This building, designed by Norman Shaw, was regarded by many as something of a monstrosity. It was replaced by the current Lloyd's Bank building in 1931, the company having amalgamated with Capital & Counties in 1918. The massive chimney stacks are the sole survivors of this Elizabethan style giant. One was re-erected on the Town Hall Buildings which replaced the Corn Exchange at a similar date, and the other now forms part of the Bush Hotel complex.

The River Wey forms the foreground to this view of Waverley recorded by John Henry Knight in the latter years of the 19th century. Stella Cottage, with its lawns sweeping down to the water, can be seen to the left, while the range

of Waverley Mill lies to the right. The miller's house is all that survives of this once great mill, but, apart from this, the scene remains essentially unchanged today, even to the wooded slopes of Camp Hill rising in the background.

Weybourne schoolhouse, built by John Henry's mother, is the central feature of this village view dating from the 1880s. On the extreme left the elm tree which stood at the crossroads can just be seen, while between the two is the pub of the same name, although an earlier building than that of the present day. Today, the schoolhouse has been converted to a private dwelling, although little modified from its original design.

John Henry Knight's children pause for a break while on an excursion from Barfield. They are at the foot of Camp Hill on the Elstead Road at Waverley, and beyond them, on the sharp bend, can be seen Stella Cottage. The latter gets its name from the lady who was romantically linked with Jonathan Swift, author of *Gulliver's Travels*, at the time secretary to Sir William Temple at nearby Moor Park House.

Village Life

An English heaven. Bourne village before its beauty became tarnished by traffic and developments.

Who can remember Farnham Blue Coaches, built at Abbotts, Wrecclesham?

Room inside ...possibly the first bus at Millbridge. It must have been a bumpy ride with those solid wheels. Frensham Pond Hotel is advertised along the side of the roof.

Wrecclesham 1950 ...the absence of traffic provides quite a contrast to today.

Ready for anything ...Elstead Fire Brigade *c.*1921.

Mr Oliver and family, licence holder of the Victory Inn (now demolished), Hogs Back, Seale. Mr Oliver was born at the Victory Inn in 1885. How did he manage with that extra little finger on his left hand?

A fine band of men ...Seale and Sands cricket club *c.*1912.

A Seale and Sands Youth Club outing about 1948.

Upstairs and downstairs and even outside staff at the Barrows, Tilford, *c.*1900.

In May 1965 the future of Tongham seemed to be in safe hands judging from this fine array of the village youth at the annual baby show held in connection with the carnival.

The Scouts of Badshot Lea parade on the village green with the schools and church in the background. Dan Finnigan, who sent in the photograph to the *Herald*, said that the picture was interesting because it places the date it was taken after the completion of the church in 1903 but before the building of the parsonage in 1914.

Young residents of Wrecclesham march along with the 2nd Battalion the Ghurkas, during the 1950s.

The Sands local taxi was owned by Ernie Gardner of Smugglers' Way. At one time he was also the owner of the village's only telephone. This was used for getting urgent messages to the district nurse who lived at the other end of the village.

A Seale school group in 1952, with teacher Mrs Grover.

Forty-five years ago, the start of a hare hunt at Crondall.

Horses and man in working harmony ...getting the harvest in at Dippenhall, 1953.

England's green and pleasant land ...the Bourne Valley 40 years ago.

It's a tight squeeze as this bus and car pass between The Happy Home and Fox Inn on Frensham Road at Lower Bourne, in 1956.

Not a film set, this really is Churt village with the Post Office on the right *c.*1900.

Young and old gather for the planting of the Edward VII oak on Tilford Green in 1901.

Pictured are all the members the Weybourne WI in 1952 when they met in a Nissen hut which served as the village hall until 1972.

This and the previous photograph were supplied by Brian Cheeseman – his mother was a member of the WI committee, shown here enjoying a cuppa.

Mr Brown and sons of Crondall, rick making in 1950.

The Tilford Horticultural Society Committee in the 1930s. Nearly all the committee were head-gardeners and under-gardeners in the village's 'Big House Gardens'.

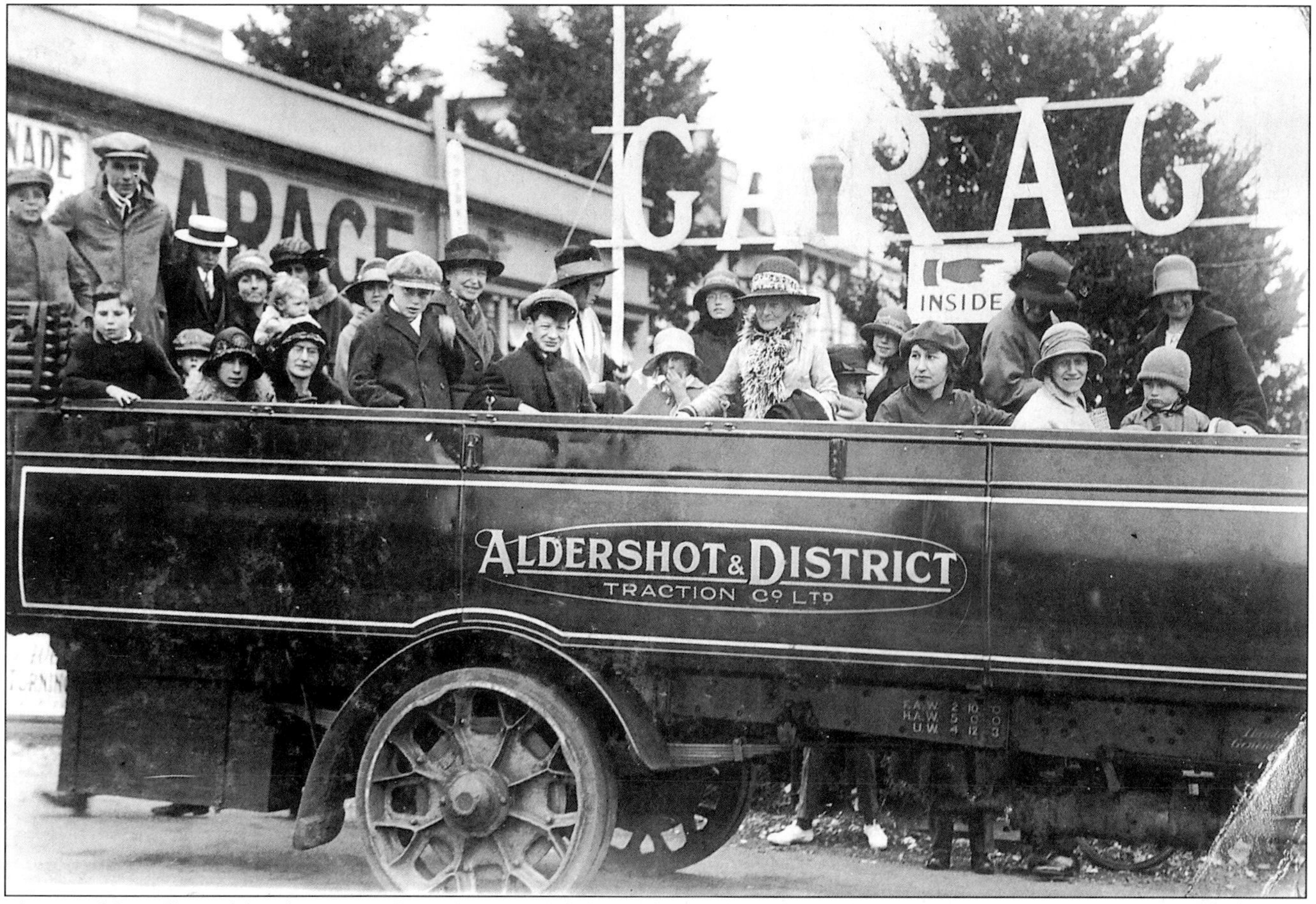

The seaside calls ...this trip to Southsea in 1928 left from the Barley Mow, The Sands.

A trip to Southsea from Seale in 1931. The Revd Arrowsmith is giving instructions about the time of the return journey.

Seale Post Office and shop was closed in the early 1970s. It was run by Mr and Mrs New, and their fat Pekingese dog was always stretched out on the counter.

The Sands shop *c.*1916, with Mr and Mrs E.Whittle and son and Mr George Warner.

When the Revd Griffiths left Seale village in 1895, a party was given in the old Rectory, now known as the Great Tythe garden.

Another trip to Southsea, and this time it's the turn of Sands Football Club in 1934.

An important day in the life of Seale and Sands was the annual fair of the Friendly Society. Here, members are at the Victory Inn, Seale. There was no shortage of hospitality as they toured the village visiting the many big houses.

As part of a lightning tour of Europe in June 1967, a party of American farming students spent 24 hours in England and, for their only visit to a farm in this country, went to Mellow Farm, Dockenfield, owned by Mr D.I.Hadfield. The 21 Americans, with the English party which included four local Young Farmers' representatives, Mr Terry Riley, Mr David Comber, Mr L.Glaysher and Miss Joan Little, are seen admiring a fine Hereford bull which was on loan to the farmer.

A group outside the Victory Inn, Hogs Back, Seale.

Manor Farm, Seale, showing the pound where stray animals were enclosed. There is now a craft centre in the buildings on the left. The main building/barn is being developed into private dwellings.

Buses await their passengers at the Shortheath crossroads. The bus on the right indicates it is Rowledge-bound. The shelter appears to offer a fair degree of comfort for waiting passengers.

Not a sport which would be tolerated today, but this group was gathering outside the Mariners, in Frensham, before heading for the river to hunt otters with their hounds.

A monster trimmed ...the Tilford oak is 'topped' in 1951.

The transport for this outing of 'regulars' from the Badshot Lea Working Men's club in 1952 was provided by Comfy coaches from the Bourne in Farnham. The fleet was run by Gudge's Garages (now Tourist Trophy). In the photograph are B.Munday, G.Cook, A.Turner, B.Clark, Ted Woolley, G.Pharo, J.Gunner, H.Gardiner, B.Matthews, B.Bright, S.Fasterne, J.Armstrong, T.Thomas, A.Butler, J.Alexandra, J.Bright, A.Bright, C.Bendall. They were obviously well prepared for a long journey, judging by the size of the beer barrel (photograph supplied by A.Bendall).

Andrew Chuter, founder of the Frensham building firm, with six of his sons, and pet dog. Much against the odds, all six sons survived their military service in World War One.

The main building of the Sanatorium, The Sands, which opened in 1900 for the treatment of consumptives. The climate, it was claimed, was more bracing than that of Bournemouth.

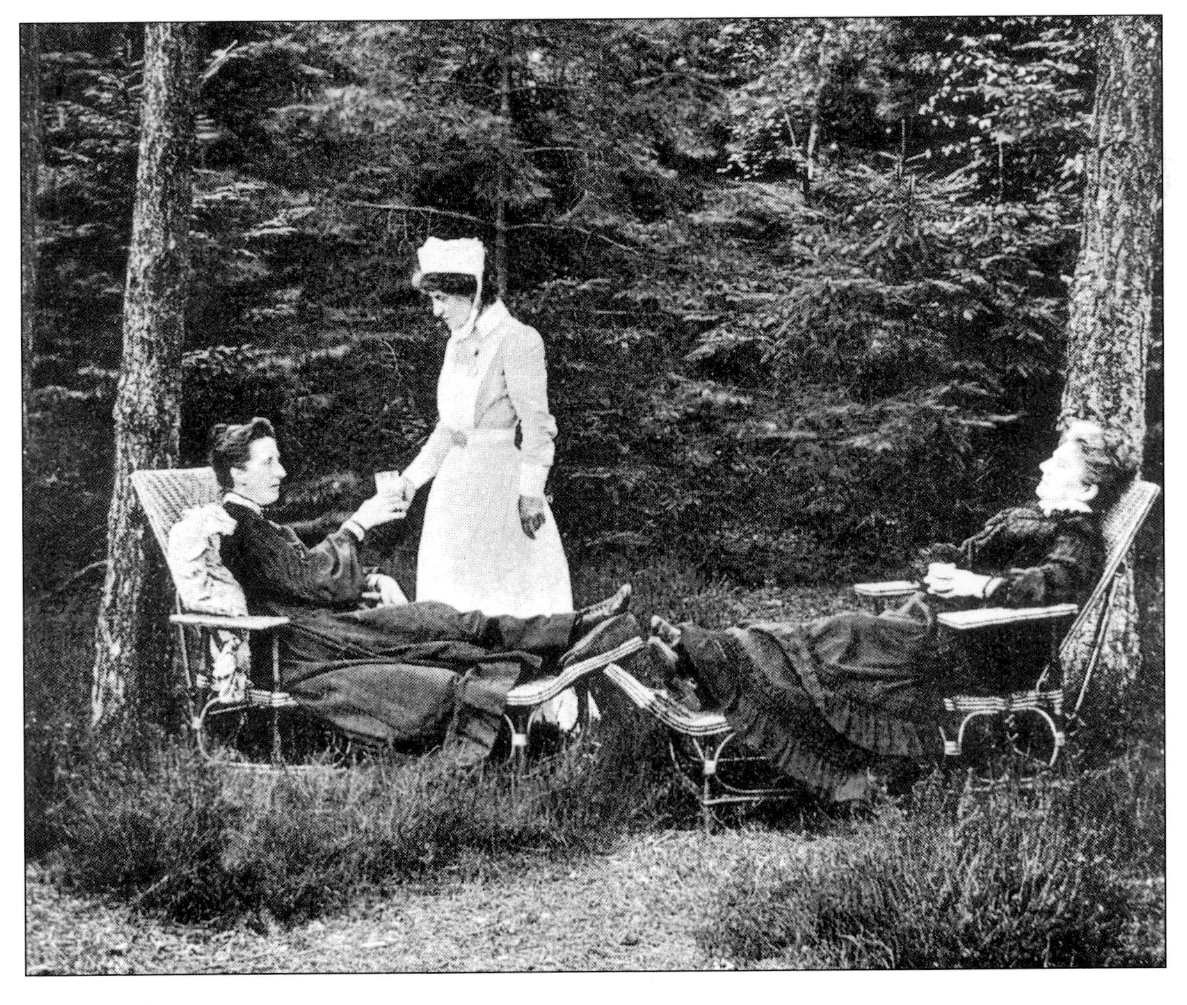

Rest hour for patients at the sanatorium at The Sands.

Troops who were camped on Frensham Common in 1914 take their horses down to the water to cool off.

Not too busy today ...pump attendants ready to serve at the Jolly Farmer filling station at Runfold.

Seale Church. This photograph must have been taken before 1917 as a further three clocks were added that year. Only the one is showing here.

Tug-of-war at a flower show held in the grounds of Froyle House – now Lord Mayor Treloar College – in 1949.

Workers of Chuter & Sons take a breather during the building of Dockenfield Church in 1910 ...and two of the brothers in the company, Tom Chuter and Harvey Chuter.

Guides parade at Churt on a snowy March afternoon in 1949.

The opening of Wrecclesham Youth Fellowship in 1949.

Getting wet in the water hazard at Wrecclesham fête, 1949.

Lady Baden-Powell inspecting guides at Pierrepont Farm, Frensham. The Baden-Powells lived at Bentley.

Mrs Atlee, wife of Prime Minister Clem Atlee, preparing to cut the birthday cake at the International Children's Home at Tilford. She is in the light suit. Lighting the candles is the French Ambassador's wife, Madame Massigli.

Bentley was the scene of the London hop-pickers annual sports.

Crowning of the 1949 Elstead Carnival Queen.

Baby show at Tongham in 1949, but this youngster can't be bothered with the judges.

Countess Lloyd George presenting prizes at Frensham Flower Show in 1949.

What price for this cucumber? The auction after Wrecclesham's 1949 Flower Show.

Children enjoying the fancy dress competition at the Hale sports of 1949.

Keep it straight there ...a ploughing match at Thursley in 1949.

That's Entertainment

Remember skiffle? These were The Lawmen, performing in the old Gostrey Club in 1956. Daphne Maddocks is on washboard.

Raising funds for the Castle Theatre, 40 years ago: the repertory company's annual ball at the Memorial Hall. From the left: Margaret Munday, Lillian Wang, Bill Clough, Heni Franklin, Jack Wing, Murree Kelly, Madge Clough, John Kelly.

A parade of elephants from the railway station heralded the arrival of the Sir Robert Fosset's circus. Part of the route lay up Castle Hill to the park and within an hour or two, hundreds of schoolchildren were at a late afternoon performance.

A scene from *White Horse Inn*, the ambitious, production of the Farnham Amateur Operatic Society which opened at the Church House on 24 January 1963. In the centre are (left to right): Peggy German, Henry Adams and Molly Medhurst.

Participants in Miss Murrell's school concert of 1952.

Mel Smith and Griff Rhys Jones ham it up for the photographer outside the Redgrave Theatre.

Saucy Kipper III, a handsome pleasure steamer entered by Mr Charles Backhurst, took first prize in the July 1959 Badshot Lea carnival procession. Riding in the bow were two bathing belles, Cheryl and Sharon Smith. Two of the oldest life-long residents of Badshot Lea, Mrs Cope and Mr Patrick, had a place of honour on the bridge and Sea Rangers stood smartly to attention aft.

A scene from Noel Coward's comedy *Present Laughter* which was presented by the Bourne Players in May 1965 at the Bourne Hall. Left to right: Norman Isham, Joe Sparrow, Ann Thompson, Brian Cole, Elsie Appleton, Paul Rowse, Margaret Ham and Cheryl Norton.

Shakespeare at the Redgrave. A youthful looking James Bolam and his wife Susan Jameson photographed with other members of the cast of *Macbeth*.

Ian Mullins' first-ever production at Farnham's Castle Theatre was *Spring and Port Wine*, by Bill Naughton, which featured a team of repertory actors who were to stay with the theatre for other productions. The Castle Theatre was extremely popular with the town, but by 1973 it was becoming dilapidated and a trust fund was created to build a new theatre and in 1974 the Redgrave Theatre opened. Pictured from left are Dorothy Edwards, Philip Trewinard, Christian Thorogood, George Waring, Sally Arez and Yvette Byrne.

Peter Laird in *The Caretaker*, by Harold Pinter, at the Castle Theatre in 1971.

Farnham Festival, 1967. Farnham Girls' Choir and Farnham Singers, with Mrs Mary Joynes, their conductor, and Mr Michael Hurt who composed the Missa Brevus which they sang during one of the evening performances.

High steppers – all members of a local school of dancing – provided cabaret entertainment at a teenage dance held at the Bourne Hall in January, 1963.

The cast of *The Woodcutter and the Maiden*, an original ballet written by two of the children of Hale Junior School, Caroline Standford and Felicity Potter. It was performed by the school at the combined Anglican and Methodist fête at Hale Place in July 1965 in aid of Christian Aid.

Seven contestants for the title of Dairy Queen at a heat held during a dance organised by the Farnham Young Farmers' Club at the Memorial Hall, Bentley, during March 1963. Left to right: Miss Delia Bennett, Miss Linda McGhee, Miss Linda Steer, Miss Margaret King, Miss Marie Barney, Miss Sally Hird and Miss Carole Millard. Miss Steer was judged the winner.

Members of the Farnham Girls' Choir gave their annual concert at Farnham Girls' Grammar School in April 1963. In front is their conductor, Mrs Mary Joynes.

Granville Saxton, pictured left, and Andrew Jarvis star in *The Critic*, by Sheridan, at The Castle Theatre in 1970. Granville Saxton's connection with theatre in Farnham continues today, although his involvement is with the education department at the Redgrave.

These two Marshall Barnes sketches will evoke fond memories of the Castle Theatre. It is now the Pizza Piaza.

Villagers of all ages were called into action for *A Midsummer Night's Dream* at Frensham, *c.*1922.

All the world's a stage. *A Midsummer Night's Dream* performed by Farnham Girls' Grammar School Dramatic Society in 1949.

The first ball of the 1949 season for Farnham Old Timers' Dance Club.

Staff at Frensham Heights School, Rowledge, exchange classroom for stage in their 1949 production of *Pygmalion*.

It Pays To Advertise

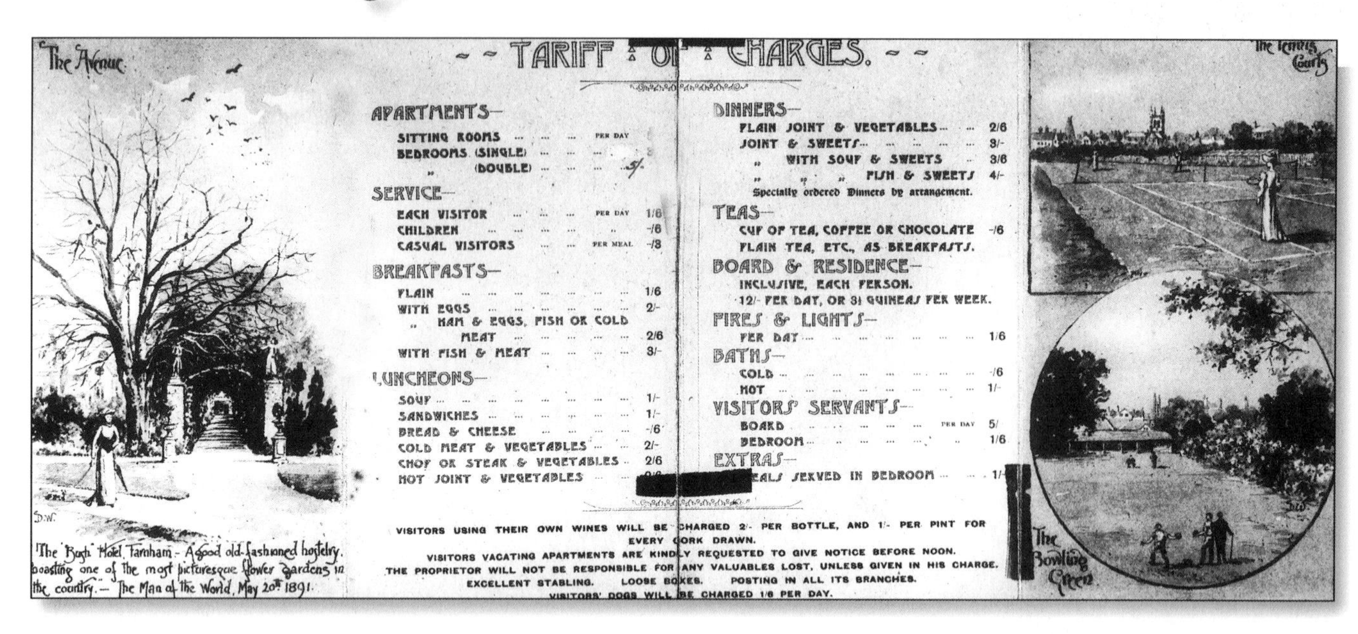
The Avenue

TARIFF OF CHARGES.

APARTMENTS—
SITTING ROOMS ... PER DAY
BEDROOMS (SINGLE) ...
(DOUBLE) ...

SERVICE—
EACH VISITOR ... PER DAY 1/6
CHILDREN ... -/6
CASUAL VISITORS ... PER MEAL -/3

BREAKFASTS—
PLAIN ... 1/6
WITH EGGS ... 2/-
HAM & EGGS, FISH OR COLD MEAT ... 2/6
WITH FISH & MEAT ... 3/-

LUNCHEONS—
SOUP ... 1/-
SANDWICHES ... 1/-
BREAD & CHEESE ... -/6
COLD MEAT & VEGETABLES ... 2/-
CHOP OR STEAK & VEGETABLES ... 2/6
HOT JOINT & VEGETABLES ...

DINNERS—
PLAIN JOINT & VEGETABLES ... 2/6
JOINT & SWEETS ... 3/-
WITH SOUP & SWEETS ... 3/6
FISH & SWEETS ... 4/-
Specially ordered Dinners by arrangement.

TEAS—
CUP OF TEA, COFFEE OR CHOCOLATE ... -/6
PLAIN TEA, ETC., AS BREAKFASTS.

BOARD & RESIDENCE—
INCLUSIVE, EACH PERSON.
12/- PER DAY, OR 3½ GUINEAS PER WEEK.

FIRES & LIGHTS—
PER DAY ... 1/6

BATHS—
COLD ... -/6
HOT ... 1/-

VISITORS' SERVANTS—
BOARD ... PER DAY 5/
BEDROOM ... 1/6

EXTRAS—
MEALS SERVED IN BEDROOM ... 1/-

VISITORS USING THEIR OWN WINES WILL BE CHARGED 2/- PER BOTTLE, AND 1/- PER PINT FOR EVERY CORK DRAWN.
VISITORS VACATING APARTMENTS ARE KINDLY REQUESTED TO GIVE NOTICE BEFORE NOON.
THE PROPRIETOR WILL NOT BE RESPONSIBLE FOR ANY VALUABLES LOST, UNLESS GIVEN IN HIS CHARGE.
EXCELLENT STABLING. LOOSE BOXES. POSTING IN ALL ITS BRANCHES.
VISITORS' DOGS WILL BE CHARGED 1/6 PER DAY.

"The Bush" Hotel, Farnham.- A good old-fashioned hostelry, boasting one of the most picturesque flower gardens in the country.— The Man of the World, May 20th 1891.

The Tennis Courts

The Bowling Green

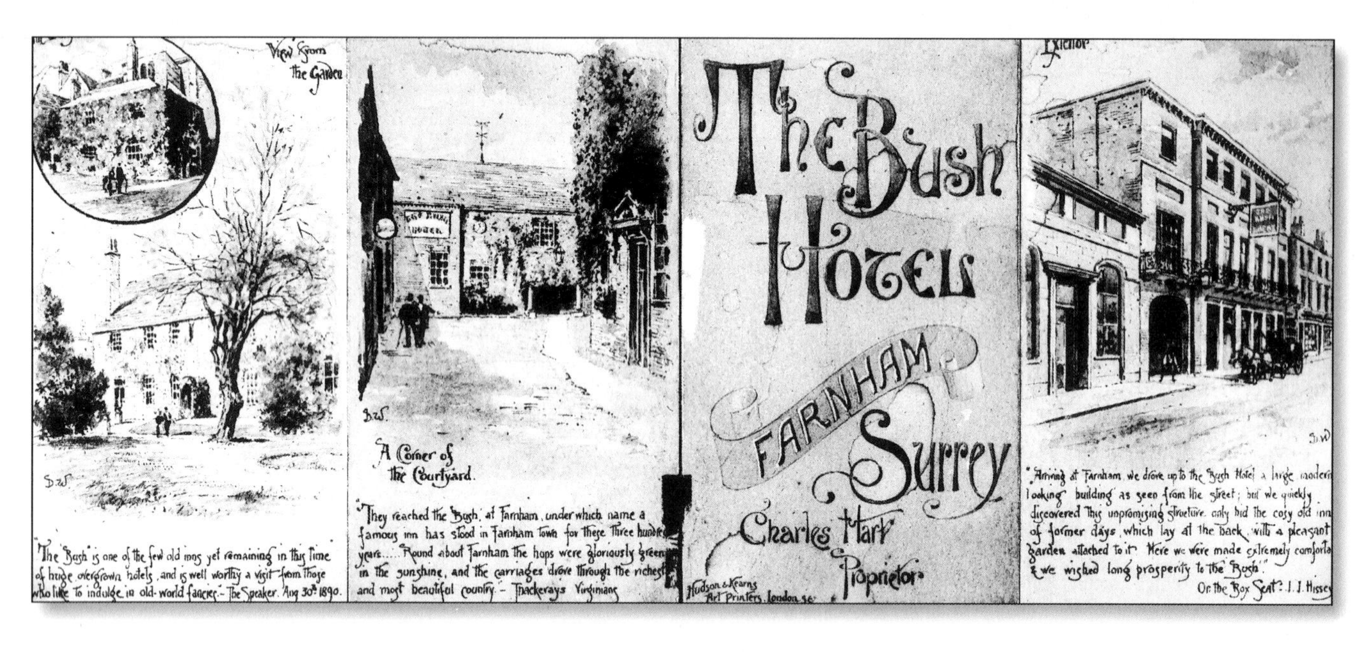

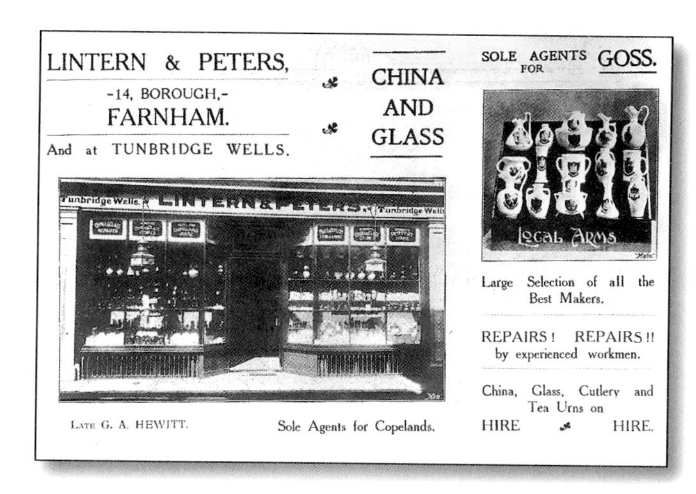

LINTERN & PETERS,
-14, BOROUGH,-
FARNHAM.
And at TUNBRIDGE WELLS.
CHINA AND GLASS
SOLE AGENTS FOR GOSS.
Local Arms
Large Selection of all the Best Makers.
REPAIRS! REPAIRS!! by experienced workmen.
China, Glass, Cutlery and Tea Urns on HIRE HIRE.
LATE G. A. HEWITT.
Sole Agents for Copelands.

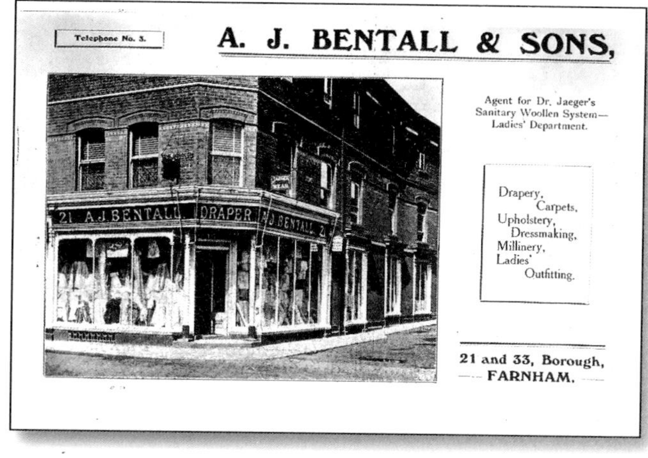

Telephone No. 3.
A. J. BENTALL & SONS,
21 A.J.BENTALL DRAPER
Agent for Dr. Jaeger's Sanitary Woollen System— Ladies' Department.
Drapery, Carpets, Upholstery, Dressmaking, Millinery, Ladies' Outfitting.
21 and 33, Borough, FARNHAM.

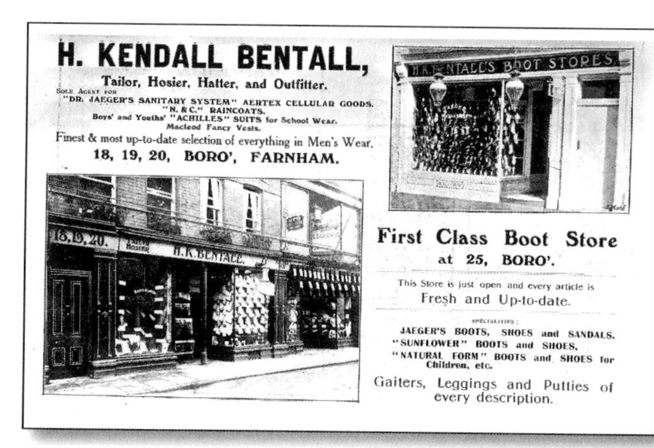

H. KENDALL BENTALL,
Tailor, Hosier, Hatter, and Outfitter.
Sole Agent for "DR. JAEGER'S SANITARY SYSTEM" AERTEX CELLULAR GOODS. "N. & C." RAINCOATS.
Boys' and Youths' "ACHILLES" SUITS for School Wear. Macleod Fancy Vests.
Finest & most up-to-date selection of everything in Men's Wear.
18, 19, 20, BORO', FARNHAM.
H.K.BENTALL
First Class Boot Store at 25, BORO'.
This Store is just open and every article is Fresh and Up-to-date.
SPECIALITIES:
JAEGER'S BOOTS, SHOES and SANDALS.
"SUNFLOWER" BOOTS and SHOES.
"NATURAL FORM" BOOTS and SHOES for Children, etc.
Gaiters, Leggings and Putties of every description.

CHARLES BORELLI AND SONS,
Established 1828.
By Special Appointment to Her late Majesty QUEEN VICTORIA.
35 & 36, Borough, FARNHAM,
Watch and Clock Makers, Jewellers, Silversmiths, and Opticians.
SIGHT TESTING by Certified Optician, F.S.M.C.
OCULISTS' PRESCRIPTIONS MADE UP.
Farnham Souvenir Goods, Spoons, etc.
Repairs of every description executed on premises by experienced Workmen.
DEALER IN ANTIQUE PLATE.

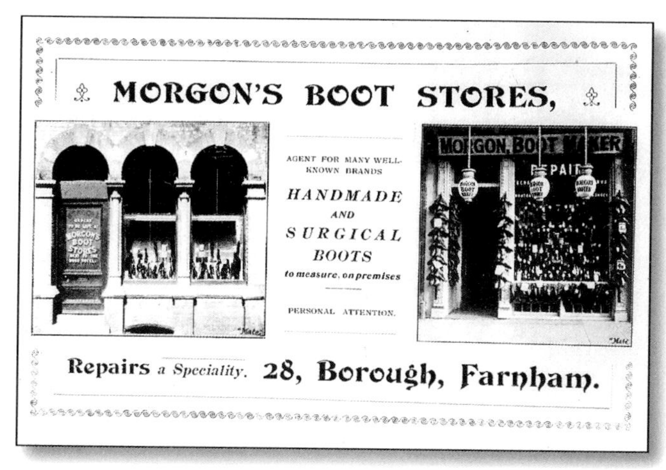

MORGON'S BOOT STORES,
AGENT FOR MANY WELL-KNOWN BRANDS
HANDMADE AND SURGICAL BOOTS
to measure, on premises
PERSONAL ATTENTION.
Repairs a Speciality. 28, Borough, Farnham.

S. BATES, 29, The Borough, Farnham.
Fruit :: of Choicest Quality Fresh Daily.
FAMILIES WAITED ON DAILY.
Vegetables
Early Garden Produce :: a Speciality.
Wreaths, Crosses, and Floral Emblems at Shortest Notice.
English and Foreign Fruiterer, Florist, and Greengrocer.

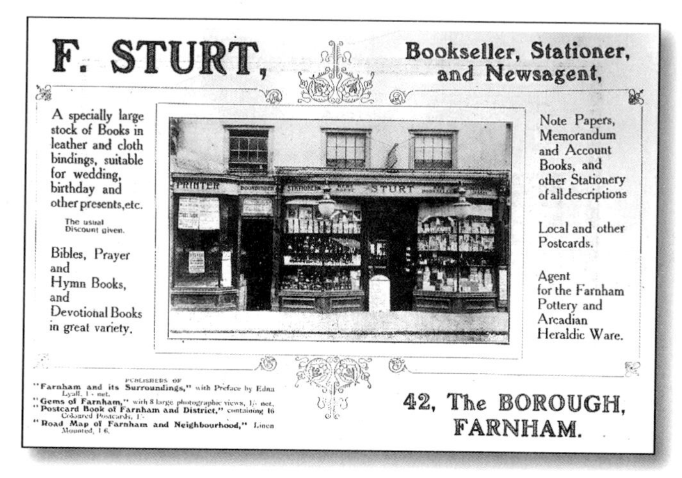

F. STURT,
Bookseller, Stationer, and Newsagent,
A specially large stock of Books in leather and cloth bindings, suitable for wedding, birthday and other presents, etc.
The usual Discount given.
Bibles, Prayer and Hymn Books, and Devotional Books in great variety.
STURT
Note Papers, Memorandum and Account Books, and other Stationery of all descriptions
Local and other Postcards.
Agent for the Farnham Pottery and Arcadian Heraldic Ware.
42, The BOROUGH, FARNHAM.

JOHN PRICE, Tea Dealer, FARNHAM, SURREY.
TEAS.
Renowned Indian and Ceylon Blends From 1/2 to 3/6 per lb.
Special Quotations to large buyers.
7 lb., 14 lb., 20 lb. Tins, Carriage Paid.
COFFEE.
Royal Pea Berry, 2/- per lb.
Other Qualities, 1/4, 1/6, & 1/8 per lb.
Price's Cocoa Essence.
30 JOHN PRICE 30
Tobacco, Cigars, Cigarettes and Briar Pipes.
PRICES ON APPLICATION.
CHINA BLENDS, 2/- and 2/6 per lb.

L. & E. WILLIAMSON,

Stationers, Newsagents and Booksellers, Fancy & Leather Goods, Toys & Games.

A splendid selection of Wools, Silks, and Fancy Needlework, and all Requisites for the same.

Newspapers and Periodicals delivered in the Town and Country.

All orders by Post receive prompt attention.
Agents for FOLEY CREST CHINA.

NOTE ADDRESS—
43, BOROUGH, FARNHAM, Surrey.

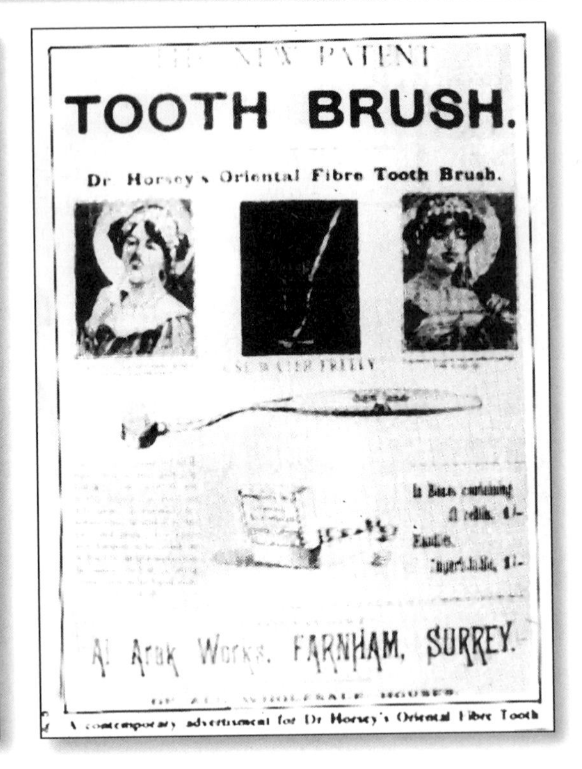

R. P. HAWGOOD,

Antique and Modern House Furnisher,

Very large stock of every kind of Furniture, Bedsteads, Bedding, Carpets, etc , both New and Second-hand.

Also a large Collection of Old Decorative China, Antique Oak Furniture, Chippendale Chairs, Old Brass, Iron Fire Backs, etc.

119, East Street, FARNHAM.

Inspection invited. Also stores at No. 17, EAST STREET.

The Farnham Dairy,

ROBINS BROS., Proprietors.

NURSERY MILK a Speciality.
THE MOST UP-TO-DATE DAIRY IN THE DISTRICT.

NEW LAID EGGS, FRESH DAIRY BUTTER, CREAM, &c.

All our Cans, &c., are disinfected and sterilized by steam apparatus, the only one in the district.

EAST STREET, FARNHAM.

Accidents Will Happen

It was no easy task for drivers, or indeed pedestrians, wanting to use Castle Hill in February, 1958.

This traction engine and harvester came to grief outside the Donkey pub at Charles Hill.

Crunch ...the aftermath of an accident at the junction of Weydon Lane and Wrecclesham Road.

This van went over at Dippenhall crossroads in 1953.

The wrecked cab of a lorry from which the driver escaped injury when it hit a tree in a three-vehicle accident in May 1965. In the picture are Mrs L.K.Lomas, wife of the licensee of the Half-Way House, and Miss Sandra Minton, of Dockenfield.

On 4 April 1931, the *Herald* reported that a large night bombing Vickers-Virginia aeroplane came to grief when engine trouble caused it to make a forced descent in Old Park, Farnham. Fortunately neither the air crew nor local residents were hurt. It must have made a very impressive sight with its 88ft wingspan, in a time when aircraft were still a comparative rarity to the man in the street. The photograph was taken by a Miss Margaret Smith who lived in Hale Village.

A Territorial Army driver and his companion experienced a hair-raising escape from serious injury when a mechanical fault occurred in the tank transporter they were manning at Beacon Hill, Ewshot, on 11 July 1958. With the two men helpless in the cab, the 21-ton unit and trailer from an RASC (TA) unit at Barnet, loaded with a 40-ton Cromwell tank, gathered speed, crashed into its turret, and only the metal roof of the transporter cab saved the two men, who later received treatment for superficial injuries at the Cambridge Hospital, Aldershot.

Happily there were no passengers aboard this No. 15 Aldershot Traction Company bus which, in 1954, overturned in icy conditions on the way down Alma Lane. The driver, Mr Rickwood, was helped out of his cab by Mr Peter Sargent, son of Mr R.M.Sargent, of St Michael's, Heath End. Neither he nor the conductor, Mr Vince of Aldershot, was injured. They were given a cup of tea at St Michael's.

Whoops! This fruit lorry drew a large crowd of onlookers when it lost contact with its load in West Street, in 1959.

Drama outside the Mariners in Frensham, youngsters look on as a steam engine tries to pull this lorry back on to the road.

A traffic island in the centre of the Farnham by-pass at Hickley's Corner was wrecked in an accident there on the evening of Thursday, 30 July 1959. A three-ton furniture removal lorry and a Bentley car, driven by Mr M.F.Gaillard-

Bundy of Wrecclesham, collided and a woman passenger in the car was taken to hospital with a badly cut knee. The picture shows the car about to be towed away.

Traffic in East Street was held up in a bumper-to-bumper stream on the afternoon of 22 April 1958, when this 35-ton boiler was being brought through the entrance to Farnham Gasworks on a trailer drawn by a 65hp tractor. Workmen struggled for three quarters of an hour to manoeuvre this huge load. The boiler was moved from Farnham to Aldershot Gasworks.

On The Streets Where You Lived

Who said traffic congestion is new to Farnham? This was the town centre scene 40 years ago. Note the two-way traffic.

Motoring bliss ...Farnham bypass, with the parish church visible in the distance.

These three pictures show diversions caused by the rebuilding of Firgrove Hill railway bridge in 1950, leading to considerable chaos on the roads.

BUS STOP
FARNHAM CASTLE STREET
VIA FRENSHAM
16
ALDERSHOT & DISTRICT
GAA 593

A busy, bustling West Street just five years after the end of World War Two.

Snow plough at work *c.*1950 as the winter weather gets a grip on West Street.

Pedestrians brave the cold and snow in Castle Street, March 1952.

A country feel in the town ...time for a chat in Red Lion Lane, 1950.

At the time of this pre-1920s photograph, the Lion and Lamb Hotel in Farnham stood empty and was offered to let by Kingham & Kingham of Aldershot. They probably had trouble disposing of the property because this is one of a series of photographs commemorating its restoration by the four Kingham brothers, Robert, Howard, Herbert and Alfred. (The photograph was loaned to the *Herald* by Terence Hembury.)

The Borough with a little more bustle, in the early 1950s.

The Borough again, in the early days of this century.

Shoppers in The Borough give their full attention to the camera, towards the end of the last century.

The Alliance, on the corner of West Street and Downing Street, was for a time run by stage star Jessie Matthews and her husband. Today it is a Black Horse estate agency.

Busy time for the vegetable stall in Castle Street, in 1950.

Taxi! It seems unlikely there was ever a shortage of carriages at the Railway Hotel.

Parking anywhere for carriages in Downing Street in 1904.

One supposes these were ladies of the highest virtue outside the Temperance Hotel on Station Road.

No shortage of hotels on Station Road ...the Railway Hotel opposite the Temperance Hotel was probably a touch livelier.

An early photograph of South Street with the council building on the right.

Flooding was quite common in the streets of Farnham, as shown here in Lower Church Lane.

Flooding in Downing Street.

The Hart in 1959, looking from West Street towards fields now occupied by Surrey Institute of Art and Design, and car parks. Modern offices now stand on the right.

The Shopping Experience

Ransom the caterers, in The Borough, was popular for lunches and afternoon teas. What's more they could take care of your garden parties!

East Street in 1916. The sign on the left advertises a 'motor works' but it's all horse-drawn traffic in the street.

The market stalls in Castle Street, around 1890. The print is taken from a glass negative owned by Dave Warner, attributed

.Knight.

The milk is loaded ready for delivery at G.Taphouse's in Downing Street.

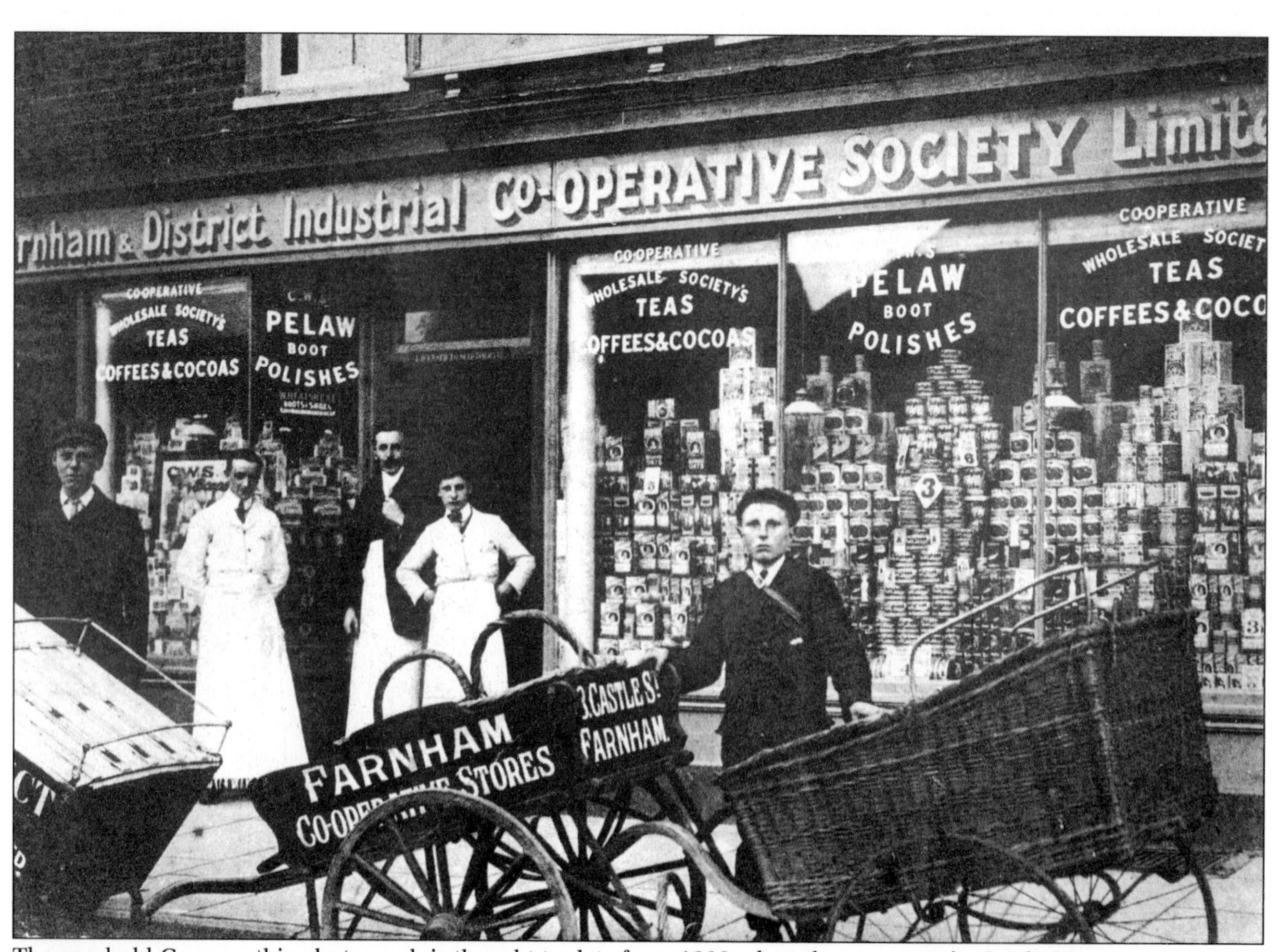

The good old Co-op …this photograph is thought to date from 1909 when the store was in Castle Street.

Clocks, watches, guns ...all to be found at Jefferys.

On parade ...the staff of M.A.Rose & Son of East Street.

Who can remember the Spinning Wheel Antiques opposite the bottom of Castle Street? This picture was taken in 1958.

Shopping brought to the doorstep ...Jim Tice's Runfold Road shop was popular 41 years ago.

Bovril and Oxo were placed in close competition in the window display at Barlings.

This photograph of Shepheard's, the general store and sub-Post Office on Station Hill, was taken in the early 1950s. Who is the toddler joining the staff for the picture? Well, that's Chris Shepheard, who grew up to become chief photographer of the *Herald*.

The same group, this time enjoying a meal inside the shop, a common occurrence it seems. And Chris? Well he seems to be camera shy on this occasion, leaning forward to be out of view.

Don't worry, Madam, we'll deliver. Blondin Brothers were among the first take food on the road.

Schooldays Remembered

The cricket team at Miss Stroud's school, Station Hill, Farnham, *c.*1910.

Pupils at Seale Church of England School in 1894. The school was built in 1849-50 and closed in 1994.

Children enjoy the early spring sunshine in Gostrey Meadow, March 1959.

The Misses Murrell's Church House School at a prize-giving in the garden of a house in High Park Road in the early 1930s.

Having a go at the tins during the fête held by the children of Wrecclesham School in aid of Oxfam. The year is 1967.

Of increasing importance in June 1965 was the annual safe cycling competition between local secondary schools, organised by the Farnham Road Safety Committee. In the picture are some of the competitors lined up in the yard of Farnham Urban Council Offices waiting for the start. A point of interest at the time was the girl, competitor No. 2, who was riding one of the small-wheel bikes.

Waiting for the coaches in June 1965. Children who attended Park Primary School, Farnham, and their parents, wait for the coaches to take them to London Airport for an outing arranged by the Parent-Teacher Association.

Wearing cardboard hats and full of high spirits, these young people thoroughly enjoyed the party held by St Francis Church (Byworth) Sunday School at St James's Hall, Farnham, at the end of January 1963.

In March 1963, a party of pupils from Weydon County Secondary School were photographed before leaving by coach for London to begin their educational cruise to Greece in MS Devonia. The ship had been charted by the Surrey Education Committee and these young people were among the 834 scholars from all parts of the county taking part in the voyage. In the front is Mrs E.M.Pearson, a domestic science teacher, who was leading the party.

The good ship Luck Dip. This model was made by the children of Tilford Primary School in the summer of 1967 for the sale they were holding in aid of extra school equipment. The portholes were marked 'Boys', and 'Girls' and 'Mixed' as a guidance to those making a dip.

Children from St Polycarp's Roman Catholic School, Farnham, crossing Tilford Road during January 1963 under the watchful eye of the crossing warden, Mr H.J.Hull, of 18 Broomleaf Road. Mr Hull's appointment followed representations made to the South-Western Divisional Executive by the school managers following a recent fatal accident to a pupil.

In the early 1920s, when this picture was taken, Hale School seems to have swept the board with sports trophies. Mrs Kath Gardiner who submitted the photograph and is now in her 80s, recalled that each year all the local schools met at the Brewery Ground in West Street, adjacent to the Memorial Hall, for the sports. Kath, then Miss Wigmore aged seven or eight, is sitting to the right of the cup table. She won the small cup in the centre of the table jointly with Arthur Larby, sitting opposite her. Others in the picture include Gwen Newman, Ivy Sparrow, May Pound, Tom Luff and Dolly Burrows.

On parade ...cadet force boys of Farnham Grammar School being inspected.

Ready, steady, dive. . . Farnham School Swimming Championships in 1958.

The heat was on in August 1959 so these schoolchildren took the chance to cool off at the town's baths.

The Farnham school sports drew a big crowd to the Memorial Ground in 1952.

All aboard ...Pierrpoint House School cadets at the Longmoor Transporation Centre in October 1958.

A group of children line up for the camera at St Polycarp's School in Bear Lane, Farnham. Undated.

August 1957 – a perfect summer scene in Gostrey Meadow.

Barfield Preparatory School, Runfold, 1940. Tom Griffith was the headmaster, and the blond boy in the middle was Mike Hawthorn, later world champion racing driver.

Hold that for the camera, please ...an intricate display staged by Farnham Grammar School gymnastics team.

Headmaster of West Street School, Mr Brooker, joins his charges for this photograph, thought to have been taken in 1910.

Steady does it ...Bill Wickens, PT instructor at St George's School, Castle Street, supervises this display to parents in 1937. There is a look of some trepidation on the faces of those youngsters waiting to be called to the makeshift balancing beam.

Hale schoolgirls enjoying their first dip when Farnham Baths opened for the 1949 season.

Some Special Occasions

Members of Farnham Urban District Council formed a guard of honour with their walking sticks at the wedding, in 1929, of hop-grower Alan Tice and Gwen Stedman, daughter of Farnham architect Arthur Stedman. Mr Tice was elected three years earlier at the age of 26 and served for 30 years. He became a county alderman.

In April 1967, the Hale Brownies, outside the Royal Arms Hotel, Heath End, cheer the royal car as the Queen drives by, having just crossed into the Farnham Urban District.

Hop pickers' wedding, September 1955. A romance which began in the hop gardens at Binsted ended in a wedding at Binsted Parish Church. The bride was Mrs Clara Hughes, of Kingsley, widow of Mr Henry Hughes, and the bridegroom was Mr Clem Butler of Andover. Interviewed outside her caravan at Mr George Retallack's farm – a red caravan, gaily picked out, with blue, yellow and green – Mrs Butler told a reporter: "My husband fell in love with me when we met at hop-picking time a year ago. He proposed on Monday and we tied it all up by Saturday." They were married by special licence by the Revd R.C.Barrass, the vicar of Kingsley. Mrs Hughes regularly picked hops and potatoes for Mr Retallack. During the war she gave her services as a fortune-teller at local fêtes 'to help the boys'.

It is 1914, it is Castle Street ...but what is the occasion? The flags indicate a certain patriotic fervour, so was it a fund-raising event for the war effort, or merely a car rally?

The Duchess of Gloucester opened the extension to Farnham Grammar School in July 1963. Pictured with her are the headmaster George Baxter, chairman of governors Alan Tice and Ernest Gudge, Chairman of Farnham Urban District Council.

Farnham Church House and the Institute Hall were hired for the old folks' dinner which was part of the King George V Silver Jubilee celebrations. There was roast beef and the 'old English beverage' of beer was drunk.

The laying of the foundation stone for Church House in 1909. The ceremony was followed by a reception at the Corn Exchange.

With World War One – they still knew it only as the Great War – still a vivid memory, this was the scene in Castle Street in 1919 as the people of Farnham gathered to remember the dead of that conflict. Farnham is often cited as being the first town to enact a two-minute silence.

In 1939, a farm cart was used to carry Richard Combes, owner of the Pierrepont estate, to his final resting place. The magnificent house is seen in the background.

Keeping spirits up ...King George V and Queen Mary visiting troops based at Frensham during World War One.

A new bird for a new age ...the first trials of a sea plane (hydroplane) took place on Frensham Pond in 1913. The craft had been brought over from Farnborough for the trials.

Whatever these were, they certainly made Castle Street look different for the Coronation of King George VI in 1937.

Farnham all dressed up to celebrate the Coronation in 1937.

One of the many street parties to mark the Coronation of Queen Elizabeth II in 1953. This is Roman Way in Farnham.

Part of the crowd who gathered to hear the declaration of the poll outside the Church House, Farnham, in 1951. Mr Godfrey Nicholson, Conservative, was the successful candidate for the Farnham Division. When Mr Nicholson's

majority of 10,198 was announced, the crowd cheered and sang *For He's A Jolly Good Fellow*. Mr Nicholson's daughter, Emma, was also a Tory MP until she defected to the Lib Dems.

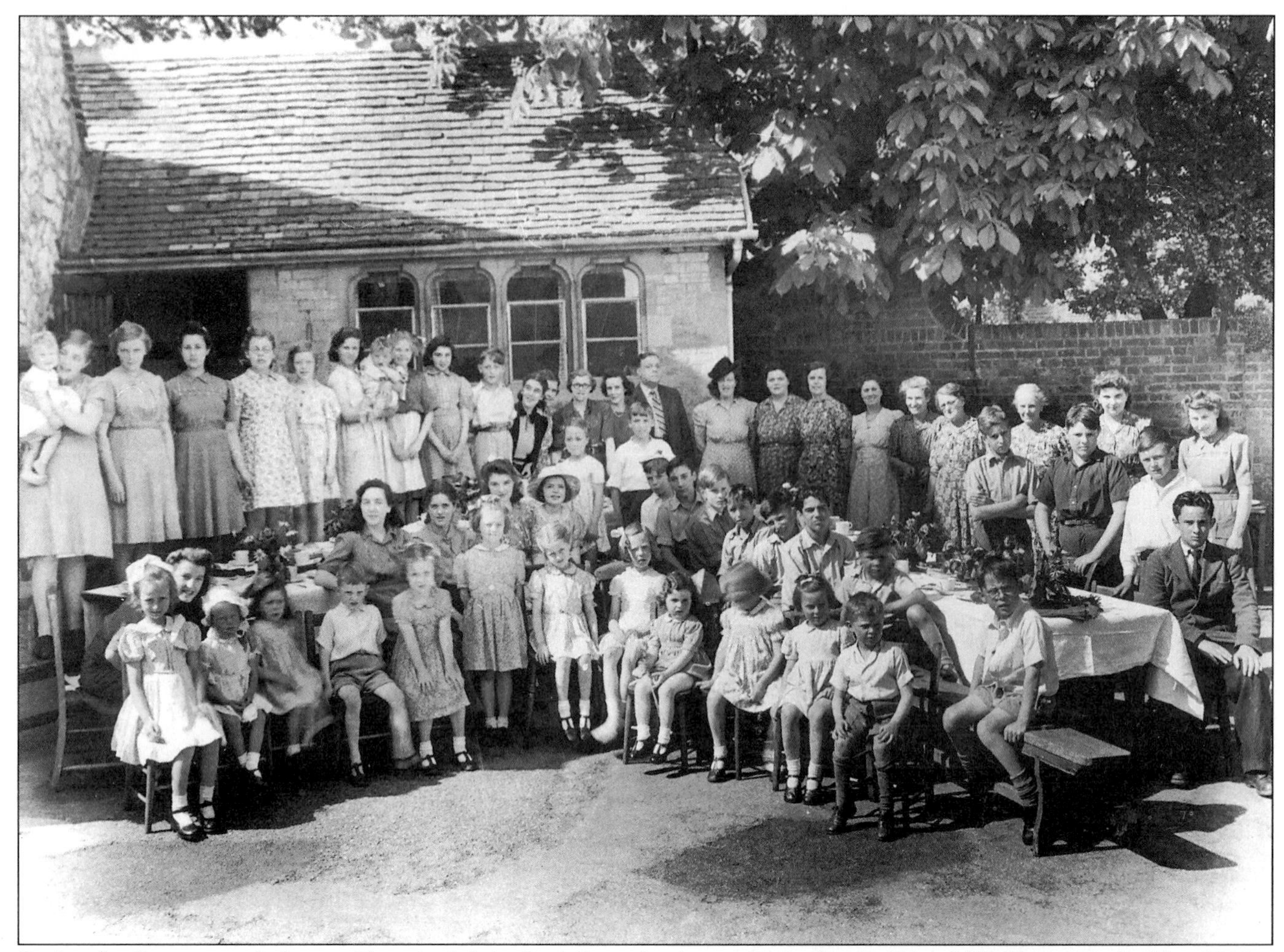

Posing for the camera before getting stuck into the jelly and cakes at St Andrew's School VE Day party in May 1945.

Parents and children gather at Elmsleigh School in May 1945 for a VE Day party.

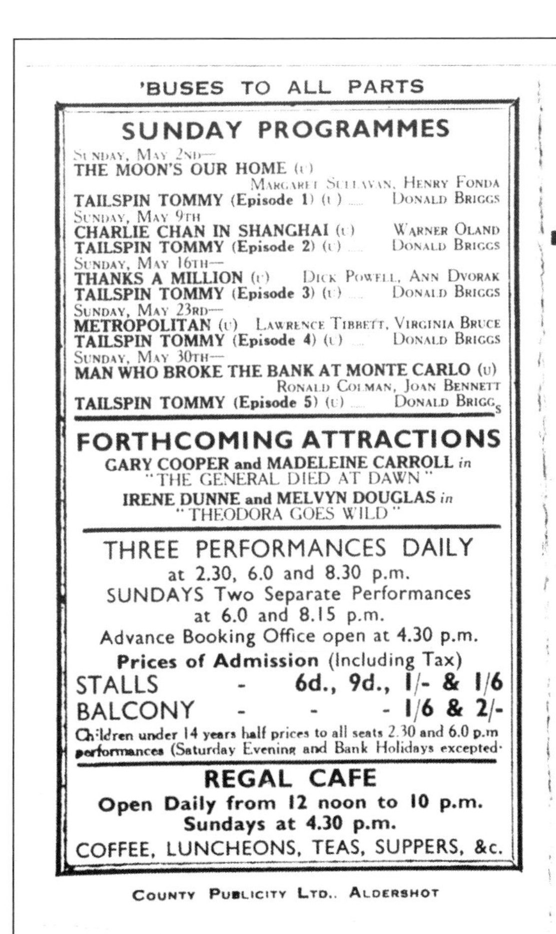

'BUSES TO ALL PARTS

SUNDAY PROGRAMMES

SUNDAY, MAY 2ND—
THE MOON'S OUR HOME (U)
MARGARET SULLAVAN, HENRY FONDA
TAILSPIN TOMMY (Episode 1) (U) ... DONALD BRIGGS
SUNDAY, MAY 9TH
CHARLIE CHAN IN SHANGHAI (U) WARNER OLAND
TAILSPIN TOMMY (Episode 2) (U) ... DONALD BRIGGS
SUNDAY, MAY 16TH—
THANKS A MILLION (U) DICK POWELL, ANN DVORAK
TAILSPIN TOMMY (Episode 3) (U) ... DONALD BRIGGS
SUNDAY, MAY 23RD—
METROPOLITAN (U) LAWRENCE TIBBETT, VIRGINIA BRUCE
TAILSPIN TOMMY (Episode 4) (U) ... DONALD BRIGGS
SUNDAY, MAY 30TH—
MAN WHO BROKE THE BANK AT MONTE CARLO (U)
RONALD COLMAN, JOAN BENNETT
TAILSPIN TOMMY (Episode 5) (U) ... DONALD BRIGGS

FORTHCOMING ATTRACTIONS

GARY COOPER and MADELEINE CARROLL *in*
"THE GENERAL DIED AT DAWN"
IRENE DUNNE and MELVYN DOUGLAS *in*
"THEODORA GOES WILD"

THREE PERFORMANCES DAILY
at 2.30, 6.0 and 8.30 p.m.
SUNDAYS Two Separate Performances
at 6.0 and 8.15 p.m.
Advance Booking Office open at 4.30 p.m.
Prices of Admission (Including Tax)
STALLS - **6d., 9d., 1/- & 1/6**
BALCONY - - **- 1/6 & 2/-**
Children under 14 years half prices to all seats 2.30 and 6.0 p.m performances (Saturday Evening and Bank Holidays excepted)

REGAL CAFE

Open Daily from 12 noon to 10 p.m.
Sundays at 4.30 p.m.
COFFEE, LUNCHEONS, TEAS, SUPPERS, &c.

COUNTY PUBLICITY LTD., ALDERSHOT

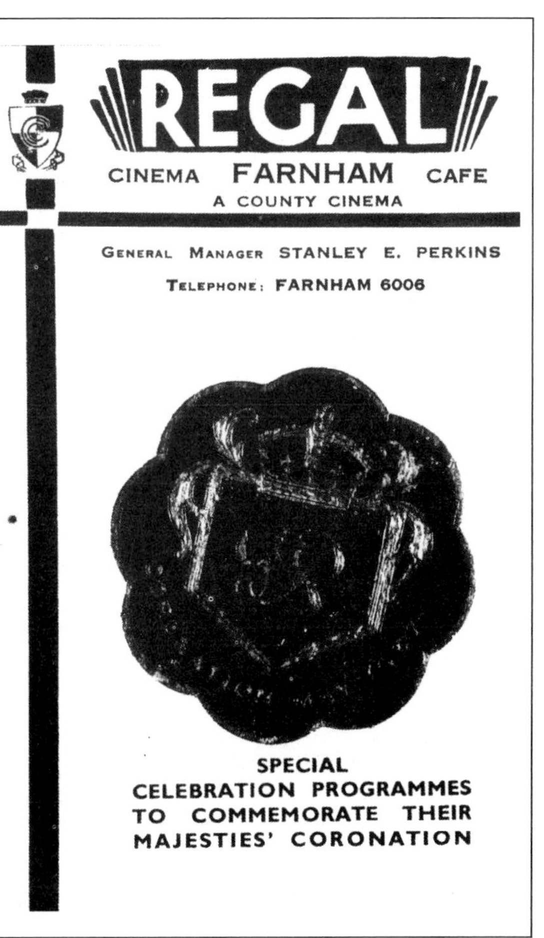

REGAL

CINEMA FARNHAM CAFE
A COUNTY CINEMA

GENERAL MANAGER STANLEY E. PERKINS
TELEPHONE: FARNHAM 6006

SPECIAL
CELEBRATION PROGRAMMES
TO COMMEMORATE THEIR
MAJESTIES' CORONATION

The Regal Cinema produced a special celebration programme to mark the Coronation of King George VI in 1937.

The Parade of Organisations swings into the Borough, heading for the Civic Service in 1953.

A Remembrance Day parade in Farnham, eight years after the end of World War Two.

In good voice for the Coronation in 1953. Community singing preceded the fireworks display in Farnham Park, leading the singers is Mr W.S.Wilkins.

Farnham Amateur Operatic Society presenting *Merrie England* in Gostrey Meadow, 1953.

Pre-aerobics days ...the Women's League of Health and Beauty step it out in the Carnival Procession during the 1953 Coronation celebrations.

Remember the Civil Defence? This was their 1953 parade through Farnham.

King George V's Silver Jubilee in May 1935 was marked by a party for children at the clinic at Brightwells Some of the children can be seen clutching their Silver Jubilee mugs.

Salute to the fallen ...Remembrance Day service at Rowledge in 1957.

Distinguished gathering at the 150th Farnham Venison Dinner in 1949.

Four years after the end of World War Two ...Remembrance Day parade in Castle Street.

Working Days

Charles Borelli supervises the fixing of the weather vane on the roof of the Town Council Offices in South Street.

A picture symbolic of the end of petrol rationing in 1950. Mr Eric Lowe, proud owner of a smart new car, and Mr Charlie Yarney, outside the Swain & Jones garage as the latter asks his customers to 'say when'.

This travelling trader was a regular visitor to the Frensham and Dockenfield areas in 1913, attracting customers with tunes on his accordion. Fresh butterscotch was considered 'grand value' at one penny a packet.

We're here to move you, sir …the Robins fleet at The Fairfield, 1954.

Frensham telephone exchange went automatic on 30 January 1963. The staff at the manual exchange were photographed before the change-over. Left to right: Mrs G.Riseborough, Miss J.Sansom, Miss J.Kinch, Miss A.Embleton, (and standing) Miss S.Poulter (supervisor), Mrs S.Haytree and Mrs S.Cooper.

It's 1958 and time for the bells of St Andrew's Parish Church to come to earth for re-casting.

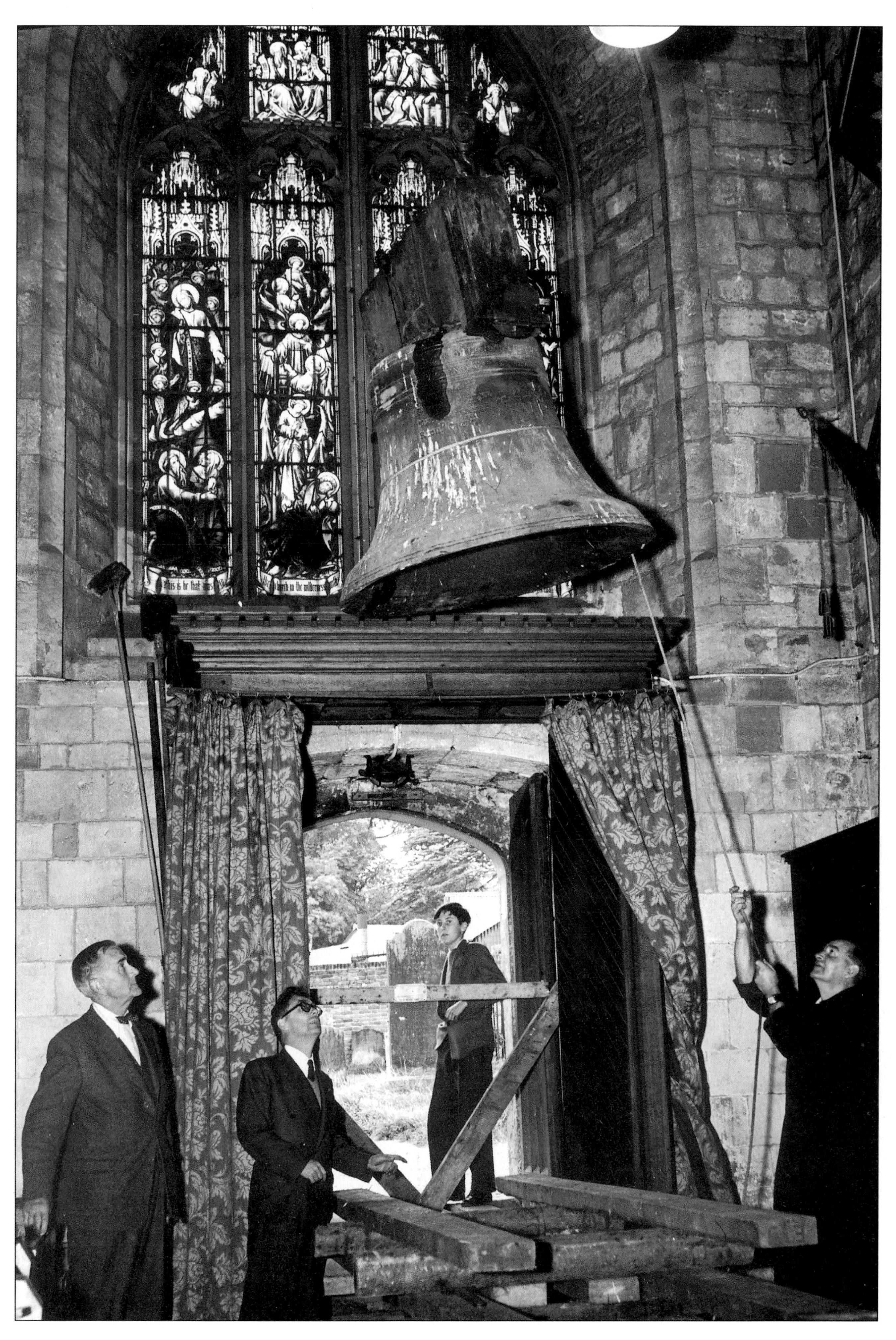
This is he that was
in the wilderness

Using a transformer to thaw out frozen pipes at a house in Castle Street, Farnham, in January 1963. An electric current is passed through the service pipe and this method enabled the work to be done quickly. On the left of the picture is Mr Adam Hope, general manager of the Wey Valley Water Company.

Time for a polish ...coaches belonging to E.J.Baker the trading estate.

Horses pulled this snow plough on Shortfield Common around 1900, watched by the village bobby. Three miles to Tilford, says the signpost, but no easy journey in these conditions.

Bread delivered to the door from Jessup & Son the Dockenfield bakers.

Standing ready to deliver ...postmen outside the Frensham Post Office before World War One. In an age when locals communicated by postcards, same-day delivery was guaranteed.

Blacksmith Walter Moulsey with members of his family at the forge in Upper Church Lane.

The *Herald* composing room in the days of 'hot metal'. In the foreground are Denis Stone, Charlie Denyer, Harold Cole and Frank Burningham.

A Mothers' Union visit to the *Herald* works in 1953. Here they see a page being assembled.

Getting into print …youngsters from Bourne School watch a Linotype operator at the *Herald* works in 1952.

Perhaps it was proving a tough day, but there was not a smile in sight from these workers at Swain & Jones garage in East Street.

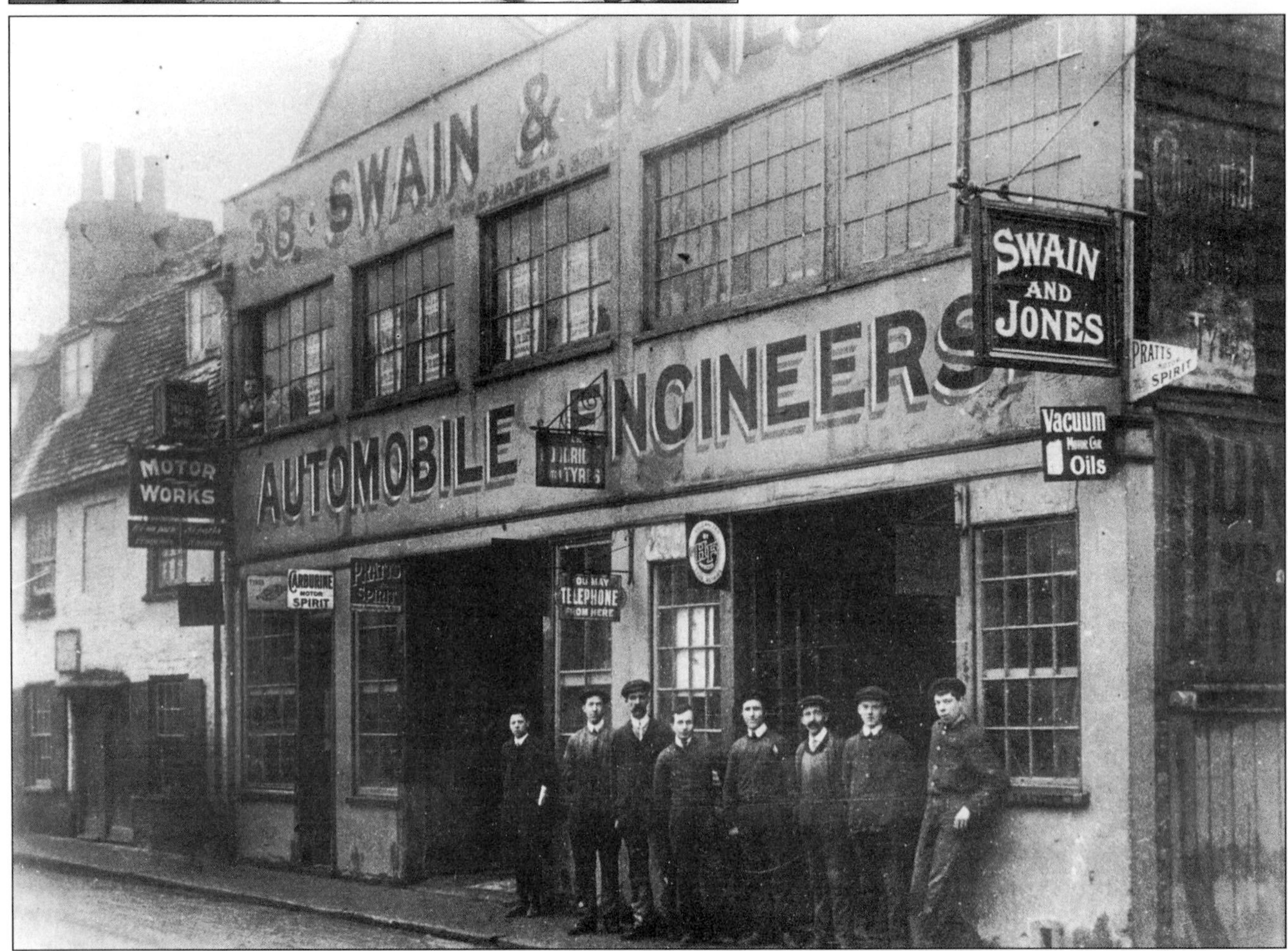

Potato pickers – thought to be at Bentley – take a break from labours to pose for the camera.

Forty years ago, tree felling in Gostrey Meadow, with the British Restaurant/Gostrey Club on the right.

Your car will be ready soon, sir ...the workshop at Heath & Wiltshires garage in 1954.

Even when there are hops to be picked, there's still time to read the *Herald*. Bide's fields in 1958.

All smiles as these workers arrive at Bentley.

Hop pickers young and old in Bide's field in 1958.

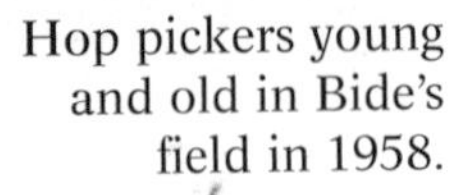

In 1953 this was a familiar and long-established part of the spring scene where hops were grown. It shows the erecting of the string frame-work from which the September harvest will hang. The photograph was taken in Mr A.R.Tice's gardens on the Guildford Road, where Mr F.C.Smith tied the strings – already cut to the correct length during the winter months – to the top wire, moving along by means of stilts. Mr T.Willis, on the ground, is tying down the strings to the middle and bottom wires. This method, carried out entirely by hand, was known as the 'Butcher system'. The 'umbrella' method – of which its name is a fair description – was a system popular in Kent. Two gangs were employed on stringing in Mr Tice's gardens. The other used a stage, a slower and less skillful method than the stilts. Mr Smith would string about an acre and a half of hops a day, and he used approximately ten miles of string (imported coir yarn) to the acre. Altogether nearly 400 miles of string were used throughout the gardens.

Beavers hop gardens in 1950. The gardens had been flattened by a storm.

Paying out time at Beavers hop gardens in 1950. Mr H.W.Bide hands out wages to Mrs Varney of Folly Hill while her fello

:kers await their turn.

Men at work ...building a post box into the wall in Bridge Square, in 1950.

Fourteen years after the end of World War Two, pill boxes in Farnham Park are blasted preparatory to being taken away.

Parcels being sorted at the Drill Hall in Bear Lane, in 1952.

Cleaning up the Wey in Gostrey Meadow, in 1953.

Snow which had been gathered up in the town and in the villages is dumped on the bypass, *c.*1950.

Some of the employees of the Old Park Brick Works, Farnham, in April 1959, shortly after owners, the Sussex & Dorking United Brick Co of Horsham, announced its closure at the end of the month. Front row (left to right): W.Chapple, L.Strudwick, R.Stokes, A.D.Watmore (foreman), H.Lewington, P.Court, W.Lodge. Back row: H.Stokes, H.Rickwood (light cap).

Last orders ...Miss Rider, manageress of Farnham Civic Restaurant, serving the last customer, Mr W.F.Browne, of Tongham, before the restaurant closed in 1953. It had opened on 16 January 1942.

Railway workers line up before a visit to the travelling Southern Railway cinema in 1953.

Before the days of double yellow lines and traffic wardens, Farnham Urban District Council workmen erect a no-waiting sign.

Waiting for a fare ...taxi drivers at Farnham Station in the 1920s. The choice of advertisement might be questioned, given their occupation!

Together for the camera, the carpenters of Goddards, the joinery works in East Street, in the early 1920s.

John Robinson, of the Sands, who was a gardener at Moor Park, *c.*1900.

Loading up from the hop fields at Bentley in 1951.

Road workers take a minute off to pose for the camera in Smugglers Way, the Sands.

No shortage of labour here ...gardeners strike an impressive pose at Moor Park House.

The entire transport fleet of William Kingham & Son lined up for the camera in Castle Street on Good Friday, 192

They also served, who worked in the field ...girls in the Runfold area.

ingham's were wholesale and retail grocers and provision merchants.

Fetching and carrying, from the water-driven Frensham mill.

Sporting Life

Not the Olympics, but still a pretty impressive opening ceremony ...Farnham District School Sports at the Memorial Ground in the 1920s.

In April 1963, Mr A.G.Hurdle presented the Borelli Cup to Newman, captain of the Hale team, after they had defeated Castle School in the final on the Memorial Ground, Farnham.

Micky Stewart, Surrey's cricket captain, shows his son, Neil, how to hold his bat, while his wife and other son, Alec, now an England player, get into the approved wicket-keeping position. The picture was taken in Farnham Park on a Sunday morning at the end of July 1965, when a Surrey Xl played a Farnham Xl for Mr Stewart's benefit – but 'rain stopped play'.

We've won! A laugh of triumph from Patricia Duckworth on winning the three-legged race at the Churt Primary School Sports in the summer of July 1965. Her partner is Alice Bower.

Pedal power ...45 years ago. Heath End Hawks cycle speedway team pose for the camera.

Not easy to stay in a straight line when you're in a hurry ...the 1951 Youth Council Sports.

Officials at the sports (left to right): Mr M.Payne (Farnham Grammar School), Mr A.H.Surman (headmaster, Weydon Secondary School), Mr J.Young and Mr R.Finbow (headmasters of Heath End and Badshot Lea Secondary Schools).

The first team of Farnham Grammar School pose for the camera in 1952.

The girls' winning relay teams at the Farnham & District Secondary Schools athletic meeting at Sheephatch, Tilford, in June 1965. Front row: (under-13) Weydon Secondary School; second row (under-15) Sheephatch; third row (under-17) R.N. School, Haslemere; back row (under-20) Farnham Girls' Grammar School.

In June 1967 the Surrey county cricket team visited Churt to play a match against the Hampshire Maniacs in aid of the David Sydenham and Tindall Testimonial Fund. Sydenham, who lived in Farnham, and Ron Tindall, the former Chelsea footballer and later manager of Portsmouth FC, both played for the county. The two teams are pictured here before the match. The Surrey players are (kneeling, left to right): M.J.Stewart (the county captain), I.Finlay, G.Roope, A.Long, R.G.Harman, D.A.D.Sydenham, R.D.Jackman, P.Pocock, G.Arnold, R.A.E.Tindall, S.J.Storey. Hampshire Maniacs are on the back row (left to right): L.P.G.Millard (umpire), R.G. Wilson, M.M.Hooker, A.G.Skinner, B.H.Lush, G.J.Cruikshank, J.Dickinson, J.D.H.Dedman, C.Portwood, M.A.R. Burchett, D.Welch, W.J.Channon, Lt-Col R.G.Buggy (umpire).

The march-past was always a feature at the beginning of the Sports Day at St George's School, Farnham. This one is pictured in June 1967.

When the BBC World Service decided to do a piece on village cricket back in the 1950s, they chose the classic setting of Tilford Green and an Anson Cup match between Tilford and Churt. In the picture Brian Johnston, later to become the doyen among Test Match Special commentators, interviews umpire Chris Harris and some players who include, from left, Gerry Morley, Michael Harris, John Charman, Frank Covey and Alf Famfield. The photograph was loaned by Robin Dibdin, a former Frensham and Churt player (far right).

The Bourne Cricket Club celebrated its centenary in 1988. This team were winners of the Farnham & District League from 1910 through to 1912.

The West Street School School football team around 1930.

This photograph was probably taken at the formation of Hale Tennis Club, before 1914. The players, somewhat overdressed by today's standards, are pictured outside the Hale Institute.

Ninety years ago ...the Farnham Post Office football team.

Seale and Sands Bowls Club team in 1959, when they were runners-up in the Hunter Cup. Pictured (back row, left to right): G.Miles, H.Doward, J.Madden, H.Smith. Front row: A.Carter, K.Binfield, H.Brown, A.Jeffreys.

Nice day out, chaps ...Farnham Road Club members pose for the camera at Selborne, around the turn of the century.

Never mind the mud, let's get on with it …the skippers of Farnham Town (right) and Leatherhead shake hands before their FA Amateur Cup match in 1949.

Double winners …Rowledge FC took the Farnham Hospital Football Cup and Farnham Junior League (Division Two) title in 1949.

Winners of the Farnham Chamber of Commerce Football Cup in 1949 were Heath End Secondary School.

Champions supreme ...the 1949 Farnham Post Office FC team won all their matches in taking the Guildford Wednesday League title, They are shown with the championship shield and other trophies.

Cricket in a beautiful setting at Hale, with Crooksbury Hill in the background.

Farnham CC first team had one of their most successful seasons in 1949.

The Rowledge cricket team of 1949 carried off the I'Anson Cup.

England, their England ...cricket in Farnham Park, 1949.

Tossing for choice of innings ...the women cricketers of Bentley and Crondall in 1949.

Winners and runners-up in the 1949 Farnham Tennis Tournament.

Nice style ...the Minister of Town and Country Planning, the Rt Hon Lewis Silkin, bowls the first wood at the opening of Elstead British Legion's new headquarters in 1949.

Mrs Danger delivering the jack to open the 1949 season at Gostrey, Farnham.

Frensham Pond, the scene of Charterhouse School's regatta in 1949.

Cycle racing was popular element of the Farnham Bank Holiday Sports of 1949.

Presentation night for the 1949 winners and runner-up in Farnham & District Darts League, held at the Liberal Club.

Ready, steady, go ...the start of a sprint at Farnham Grammar School Sports in 1949.

People and Places

The women's detachment of the Farnham Division of the Red Cross pose for the *Herald* photographer in 1949.

No kidding, Mr Hitler ...these concrete pillars were planted in Farnham Park to prevent enemy aircraft landing.

Monty in town …Field Marshal Viscount Montgomery, who lived for many years at Binsted, leaving Farnham Post Office in 1949 after collecting his first pension.

A Grayshott British Legion Arnhem Night gathering four years after the end of the war.

A recruiting march through Farnham by the Territorials in 1949.

Star turn ...stage and screen performer Miss Jessie Matthews chats with the old folk at a St James home fête in 1949.

It's all eyes on the rabbits at the Farnham tables show of 1949.

Cake cutting at Farnham Darby and Joan Club in 1949.

The 1949 dinner of Brightwell Bowling Club in Farnham.

Well done, dad ...this youngster has a good view as his father receives a prize at the Farnham Parents' Association fête of 1949.

New workshops for the handicapped were opened at Woodlarks, Farnham, in 1949.

Youngsters watching an artist at work in one of Farnham's cobbled yards, *c.*1950.

Heading for some sea air ...Farnham old folk gather for a day out at Southsea in 1949.

Godfrey Nicholson, long-serving local Tory MP, addressing a gathering in the garden of The Grange, Farnham. He was the father of Emma Nicholson, who in 1996 defected from the Conservatives to Liberal Democrats.

Holding bouquets, Miss Greta Gynt (left) and Miss Evelyn Laye attending the Hale Conservative fête of 1949.

Farnham Ladies Circle hold a charter dinner in 1949.

Farnham's Safety First Week in 1949, with children showing how to cross the road.

Farnham St John Ambulance wine and cheese party at Runfold House in 1960, when the president, Alan Tice, announced an appeal to raise money for a new ambulance station.

The women's section of the Farnham TA, photographed at camp in Bude in 1953. In the second picture they are joined by the chaps, this time at their Guildford Road headquarters.

Councillors and officials join in the opening of the new canteen at the Young Farnham Youth Club in 1958. Councillor Alan Tice is enjoying a cup of tea.

Bernard Cribbins (kneeling), the stage and television actor, after opening the fête held in June 1967 at the Farnham Training Centre for the mentally handicapped. With him are two children who attended the centre, Jane Quinn and Jonathan Moore, who presented a bouquet to Mrs Cribbins (right). Centre is Mrs Templeman, the principal of the centre, and left is Mr R.Black (chairman, parent-teacher association).

Caught in the act ...where do you think you're going with those, my friend? Farnham's very own world motor racing driving champion, Mike Hawthorn, challenges legendary spiv Arthur English at a function in 1954.

Hoping to impress the judge ...the Southern Counties Goat Show field at Farnham Cattle Market in 1958.

Pop singer Pip Hinton hangs her lucky coin on the Christmas tree at the fête which she opened in June 1967 in aid of the Estead Parent-Teachers Association. With her is Mr F.F.Foster, chairman of the association and the headmaster of the primary school.

Pop singer, Chris Farlow with a police escort, but surrounded by autograph hunters, when he attended the Rowledge Methodists' Fayre at the end of April 1967.

Your country needs you! A recruitment meeting in Farnham in August 1914.

A photograph of officers and men of TS Swiftsure, Snauslynch, in 1947.

Canadian soldiers from the Alberta Regiment were billeted in Aveley Towers, Aveley Lane. Here they meet the locals at the Fox pub in Lower Bourne.

A favourite walk for locals in the early days of the century ...the old hop kilns and River Wey.

Could these men, turning sprouting barley at Farnham Maltings in the 1950s, ever have imagined that the building would one day become a community and arts centre?

The Maltings before work began on the conversion ...and then the trees are gone, allowing work to begin in 1969.

Surrey Guild of Bell Ringers members admire the view from the top of St Andrew's Parish Church tower in 1952.

The closure of a footpath in Moor Park sparked an angry protest *(Above)* and these workers from urban and rural councils *(Below)* became the heroes of the hour by breaking down the chains which were intended to deny access to the public.

And so to the present ...Farnham from the air showing Castle Street, Downing Street, the Maltings, and, yes, all those cars.

Subscribers

Barbara Myrtle Josephine Ambridge
Mrs J. Amor
Mrs Maisie Anderson
Peter and Luciana Arundell-Smith
J.A. Ash
Dr and Mrs A.J. Austin
Mr & Mrs T.J. Ball
Colin Banfield
Phyl and Steve Barnes
A.Barrow
P.A.R. Bartlett
Anne Beadle
Bill & Joan Blackman
David Blackman
Bernadette Blower
Stella Bolt
Christopher John Bonner
Miss Jenny Bray
James Brown
Roger Burge
Malcolm Casentieri
Peggy Chapman
Mrs Cicely Clark
Mr and Mrs D. Coleman
John M. Cook
Olivia Cotton
Mervyn James Court

Maureen Covey
The Coyle Family
Steve Crawte
Margaret Daniels
Norman Davies
William G. Day
Susan Dinapoli
M.C. Dunne
Fred Eagle
June Carol Edwards
Della F. Elkins
Frederick O. Elkins
Eve and Martin Fausset
Hubert D.W. Finch
Julian Fry
M.J., C.M. Garland and Family
E.Gascoigne-Pees
Betty Gaymer
Jennie Gaymer
Miss V.E. Green
Mr and Mrs E.J. Grimes
Winifred Hélène Grosset
Mrs I. Hack
A.M. Harrington
Joan and Gordon Harris
Robin Hatt
Pamela Hawkins
Mrs P. Hawkins
Mr B.V. and Mrs P.J. Hicks
Mrs Peggy Hobbs
Mr Ian S. Horton

N.J.B. Houston
Raymond John Hutchings
Mrs M.M. Jones
Mabel L. Knight
Mrs Rene Knight
Tony and Jan Knight
E.H. Lathey
Kevin Ledgerwood
M.J. Leverett
David McKenna
Wendy Maddox
Mrs L. Maher
Christopher Mansell
Mrs Vivienne Mansell
E. Marlow
M.A. Marlow
A.J.A. Mason
Irene G. Mason
Mr and Mrs P. Meere
S.J. Mew
G.S. Mew
D.J.A. Mew
E.C. Moody
Mr and Mrs W.J. Morrogh
Major N.J. Nichols
Ann Norris
N. Orchard
J.L. Park
Jean Parratt
Sandra Philpott
Vera Piper (neé Bryant)

D.L. Precious
Sydney H. Reeves
C.G.W. Roberts
F.L. Roberts
Nigel P. Robinson
Fred Rogers
H.E. Rogers
P.E. Searle
Ben Sharpe
A.M. Shergold
Brian Small
Brig. W.A. Smallman
Grace Margaret Smith
Mrs O. Sparrow
Miss J.V. Stallard
Mrs Barbara Stevens
Marion Stockley
Peter Stroud
Gavin and Marcie Terman-Smith
Sandra D. Thorns
H.J. Timson
Anthony Brian Varney
Michael Waite
B.E. Webberley
Kenneth C. West
B.J. Wheldon
Buster Wills
Babs Wiltshire
Mrs Marion Young (neé Parratt)
Valerie Y. Young